SMALL BUSINESS MANAGEMENT & MARKETING ESSENTIALS

A Guide for Small Business Owners – Evaluate your Company – Evaluate yourself – Learn and get ideas to Improve and Change

By Alvaro A. Santizo M.

Table of Contents

Your Company's Gross Profit
Gross Profit — Gross Margin - Markup

Pricing your Products or Services
Discounts
Pricing Strategies
Profit Margins
Pricing Based on Value
Pricing Flexibility
Pricing Tactics
Making Changes in your Pricing Strategy

Business Plan Basics
Business Plan Structure

Small Business Marketing Essentials
Getting Organized
Exercises and Check Lists

PROLOGUE

THERE MAY BE MANY REASONS WHY A SMALL BUSINESS CAN FAIL...AND TO ME, THE MOST IMPORTANT ARE:

Reason #1: Business Owners are not really in touch with customers through deep dialogue. They do not know their needs and how they evolve.

Reason #2: There is no clear and real differentiation in the market, they have now unique value proposition and as almost every small business owner they try to compete based on pricing.

Reason #3: The Failure to communicate value propositions in clear, concise and compelling fashion. Commonly mistaking advertising with a marketing strategy.

Reason #4: Leadership breakdown at the top. Yes....business owners have trouble being leaders, and building the right team needed to accomplish their objectives and goals.

Reason #5: Inability to establish a profitable business model with adequate financial indicators. (Are you the type of owner that mixes personal and company finances?)

If you can identify with one of the reasons, I need you to ask yourself...

Is your business facing challenges?

Do you have adequate financial management practices? Financial Indicators?
Do you have a business plan? A Marketing Strategy?
Do you know the industry and the market?
Are your profits at risk? Do you monitor and control your expenses?
Do you use cash flows and budgets? Does that information help you make better decisions?

How do you monitor performance? Do you have the right team to achieve your goals?

Are YOU ready as the leader?

Are you motivated? Organized?
Do you monitor your performance and profitability?
Are you a good leader? Do you have high personnel rotation?
Are you reaching your personal goals being a small business owner?
Is your company designed for YOUR wellbeing?

If you are here, you already own a small company or you are about to start your own business, either way, this book is designed to help you learn about critical topics needed to manage and succeed when you are a small business owner.

You may already know that the value of what you offer in a small business is based on your skills, your vision, and what you want to accomplish. You will be the one setting the goals for the company, and you are the key ingredient in the company's success.

You might have a special skill, a quality or knowledge that will set you apart from the competition, but in every business, that is just a small factor that can influence if you succeed. Your knowledge, education and experience can guide you to start, but there are areas within a business that you may not be completely aware of. And this course is designed to help you gain perspective on the different areas within a business, so you can evaluate and implement changes in your project or company.

Understand that every small business, no matter the industry, has a risk of failure, and that will depend on many factors. Not only your knowledge, skill set, experience and desire, but other areas that you might not control, or are not aware how to handle.

Is there a way where you can minimize that risk? **Yes,** you can be prepared from the beginning or have the ability to correct the course of action if you are already started.

No matter what you have done with your company, or what you plan to do with your small business, let me tell you something right now, you are an admirable person for doing this, or wanting to do it. You are a difference maker and you will succeed no matter what. Either you achieve the success you desire, or learn what it takes to do it. And no matter the outcome, that requires a quality that few people have.

Let me be clear, if you are a small business owner, or become one, you will be the most important asset to start, but as you prepare to gain experience, you have to be subjective to your own strengths and weaknesses.

After you finish the book, it will allow you find areas where you can improve an existing business or prepare to start one This book will help you identify critical tasks and areas within your company that you need to evaluate. We will do exercises and tests that will allow you to learn about small business finances, being a leader, marketing, hiring the right team, be organized and help you improve the chances of your company becoming successful.

CHAPTER 1

Knowing your business

- Do you have what it takes to manage a small business?

- Ok so you have decided to venture on your own. You want to start a company or already have one and you already or want to lead a group of people based on your vision, goals and objectives. But, are you certain you have every quality needed to lead that team to success? Are there any areas where you might need assistance?

- If you made the choice to start your own business, you are an entrepreneur. Your background, your education, your skills and capability will define how far you go and how quickly you can reach your goals.

- The different levels of knowledge, skill, desire, preparation and all the factors involved in starting, owning and running a business will determine how long it takes for you to get it right. You might be a doctor, veterinarian, architect, chef, or a high school graduate with an idea for a product or service. You might have learned something in school or in life that made you excel in an area you are passionate about.

  But a reality that you must know now, and as an entrepreneur you should always be conscious about: "You cannot know and do everything on your own."

  - If you are a doctor or veterinarian, you know how to diagnose, heal and help patients regain or maintain their health. – If you are an architect, an app developer, or a web designer, you know how to design, evaluate functionality, be creative and so many other things that will help you distinguish yourself in a specific field" but to start, maintain and run a business, you need a lot more.

- It does not matter how you started the business, or if you are about to start one, you need to understand that running a small business requires more than just a good idea, service or product. It is imperative for a small business leader to be aware of their capabilities as the manager, owner and more importantly, be conscious about the limitations that might put the company at risk.

Am I ready to lead a small business?

Understanding situations, and problems you might encounter being a small business owner might allow you identify areas where you need help or change. Being aware of your capabilities is an asset, but not knowing your limitations or deficiencies can create a difficult work environment and put your company´s future at risk.

Am I ready? The following questions are some aspects you need to evaluate about yourself, be honest in your answer and identify areas where you can improve.

- Based on your life experience, are you a follower or a leader?
  a) I have always been a leader
  b) I have been a leader but also a follower (I can recognize good leaders)
  c) I have always been a follower

- Are you good in making decisions? Can you handle making bad decisions?
  a) I can make decisions and accept consequences (good or bad)
  b) I can make decisions but have trouble accepting consequences.
  c) I always consult and over analyze and have a hard time making decisions.

- Have you ever quit something you started? Have you always achieved your own goals?
  a) I have never quit anything
  b) I have started and kept going for a while but after my interest changed I quit
  c) I have quit many times

- Do you accept responsibility or blame others?
  a) I have always been responsible for my actions.
  b) Sometimes it´s not I, the circumstances of the situation can change.

c) When most things don´t go as planned, it is not my fault.

- Are you a good planner?
    a) I can develop strategies and plans without assistance.
    b) I have trouble defining specific tasks sometimes.
    c) I have ideas but I find it difficult to list the tasks needed to achieve them.

- Can you organize multiple tasks and be responsible of their advancement?
    a) I can follow tasks and advancement with ease.
    b) I can set tasks without a problem but I do not follow up.
    c) I have problem following steps and guidelines and are easily distract myself with new tasks.

- Are you self-motivated? Do you need approval from others to feel good about your decisions?
    a) I convince myself easily about projects or ideas and seldom seek approval.
    b) I can get excited easily about my ideas but I need someone to validate me.
    c) I have a hard time keeping up my motivation with or without approval from others.

- If you planning to start, or already own a small business, what is your goal? What do you want to achieve?
    a) My goal is clear and I am on my way to achieving it.
    b) I am not sure about my goal or how to achieve it.
    c) I do not know what I want to achieve and my goal is unclear

- Do you get along with others even if you disagree? Can you respect different opinions or ideas?
    a) I can get along with anyone, even if I do not agree with their opinion or ideas
    b) Sometimes I am able to respect other people´s opinions but I do not vary my opinion and sometimes have trouble working with others.
    c) I have trouble respecting people who do not agree with me

- Are you punctual and responsible with dates?

a) I am always punctual with appointments, payments, dates and anything I am responsible for.
b) I am usually on time and responsible.
c) I have trouble managing time and dates.

- Are your personal finances in order?
    a) I have little to no debt, I save and I am always punctual with my financial responsibilities, my credit score is excellent.
    b) I have accumulated debt but I seldom miss payments and my credit score is acceptable.
    c) I have trouble keeping up with my financial responsibilities and my credit score has suffered because of it.
- Are you trustworthy?
    a) My actions reflect my words and I always deliver my promises.
    b) I have good intentions with everyone but sometimes I find it hard to execute and deliver.
    c) I like to promise to make people feel good, but I rarely deliver my promises and just move on and forget.

After you finish your test please list the number of answers you chose based on the letter selected:

Number of answers you chose A:

Number of answers you chose B:

Number of answers you chose C:

DO NOT ADVANCE TO THE NEXT PAGE BEFORE TOTALING YOUR ANSWERS ACCORDING TO THE LETTER CHOSEN.

Now based on the number of total answers you have on a), b) and c).

If most of your answers are a) they you have a great base for leading and managing a company. If your answers are mostly b) and c) then you might have more trouble than you can handle by yourself. In such case a partner might be an option to evaluate. And be conscious of where you lack the abilities that might limit your opportunity to succeed. If needed, seek assistance, learn about the areas where you can improve. That will allow you to be better prepared for what it takes to run a successful business.

Is my business ready?

The following questions are some aspects you need to evaluate about your company or idea, be honest in your answer and identify areas where you can improve in your business structure.

1. Do you have a business plan? Why do you need one? Is it up to date?

   o A business plan is a complete document that will detail how a new or existing business will achieve their objectives and goals. I helps you define and measure results, set guidelines for strategy and indicators of where you want to go and how to get there.

   o The components of a business plan include your financial information, balance sheet, income statement, cash flow, projections or results, market study, a marketing strategy and all the resources and information needed to handle your company's operations and make the right decisions.

   o This document can guide your personnel, your suppliers and anyone interested in participating or working in, or with your company. It can easily trace operations, objectives and help you in the path to your ultimate goals.

- A business plan is essential to determine why and how your business will succeed and it is a crucial part if you ever want to apply for a loan. Either for a startup or an operating company planning on growth expansion or traditional business loan.

- This will provide you a map and overview of how well adapted you are to changing market conditions. If you want to grow, a business plan is essential to helping you.

2. Have you defined your business in detail?

- If you are already operating or evaluating your plan to open a business you need to consider and ask yourself: "What business are you really in?"

The importance of this question before you start, or as you are evaluating your company, is essential to what you will accomplish. Consider all the companies that have gone out of business because they were unclear of what they were actually doing.

For example, a company I worked with, represented worldwide manufacturers of hardware and software, and sold licensing, installations, and provided technical services and training to all types of companies. From small to giant multinational companies. When they called me to assist them because they had a difficult couple of years, my first task was to evaluate the results of their different divisions. How much income did they generate selling hardware and software licenses? How much did they generate installing equipment, and how much did they generate providing technical services? The company owners and founders where IT graduates, software people, certified, brilliant, and with a great name and history in the market. But they did not realize small details like these. The hardware and software licenses they sold required specialized sales reps, very expensive personnel, and the margins in hardware and licensing can be very competitive and low. The sales numbers on installation and services were lower, but the margins were impressive. But they promoted themselves as a hardware and software licensing company, "if you want to buy a new computers, servers and programs for your company and all your employees talk to us". And they advertised it, and the sales rep earned huge salaries, but they did each rep did not sell enough software to pay even their own base salary.

The hardware helped cover the cost of them, but it was very competitive and big sales were not frequent. As I continued to analyze I determined the cash to operate the company was coming from the services, trainings and installations. The technicians that programmed, installed and provided tech services cost the company a lot less than sales reps and the amount they generated per month was a lot more profitable than selling hardware and software. Selling hardware and software almost led them to be bankrupt. And after the evaluation, they still sold it, but as a byproduct of services. They promoted themselves as a leading tech services, installation and training company and that is just what the clients needed. In one year we increased overall sales by over 35%, but more importantly, cut costs by over 20% (not as many sales reps needed) and profits over 50%.

As you can see, that example can apply to a lot of small businesses that try to do a lot and not focus on what it is good and profitable for the company. Defining your purpose clearly can help you establish a sense of direction while your company and business develop.

3. What resources do you have to achieve your plans?
    ○ Are your plans clearly defined and is the timeline set on what you want to achieve, and how you will do it?
    ○ If you have plans or ideas, can you put them into action immediately?

Establish your resources:

Do you have the right personnel?

In the different areas of operation in a small company, there might not be a lot of people when you begin, but there will be a lot of tasks. As the owner, what will be your responsibility? Do you have the tasks and objective clear? If yes, do you have the right personnel in the right position?

You have to be certain that they deliver what you ask, and are100% clear on what you want to achieve.

If needed, you have to provide the training, a clear job description or the incentive needed to attain the results you seek. If you are clear about what everyone will do, determine if it is enough or if you need to subcontract part of the services you need to execute the plan.

-   Are your suppliers meeting your expectations, or can something be improved?

    Part of your plans might involve cost reduction, or supply chain efficiency. Because of that you need to evaluate your suppliers. They are your business partners you depend on to deliver a high quality product or service.

-   Do you have the economic resources to execute your plans? Have you made a real budget, cash flow, projections and forecasts to establish your needs? What kind of access do you have to credit, or will you use your own savings? – Whatever the plan and analysis, have you established a payback period on the initial or required investment?

4. Is your market ready?

-   You have defined your product or service, you excel at it and are completely certain that you can achieve success. For this to happen, you need to understand your market. It doesn't matter if you are on the planning stage or if you have been at it for years. It doesn't matter if you are on the planning stage or if you have been at it for years. If you are unaware of your market, the trends and what you require to gain and retain customers, you will not be able to grow and may even fail.

Markets evolve and change constantly. The trends can vary with consumer habits, new competition, new technology and how the business operates.

- Regardless of what stage you are in your business, you have to be up to date, aware of your demographic, know your costumers and their needs.

5. How is your financial structure?

- The growth and longevity of a business depends on financial management.

  - Are you aware if your financial management practices are strong?

  - Do you analyze and control your cash flow? Is it healthy?

  - Are you on top of your suppliers? Have you over paid for any materials or services?

  - Can you improve profit margins by reducing costs or improving your pricing strategy?

  - Do you track your sales to help you make business decisions?

  - What are your financial key performance indicators? (KPI's)

- It is irrelevant if you manage your finances in house or if you sub contract financial services, you need to know the system being used and discuss it with a professional to establish if there are options to improve it. If you plan to grow, you need to handle the financial aspects of your business at an advanced level. Establish the necessary conditions to learn the systems, and develop all the layers in financial management.

6. Are you aware of all regulations in your business? Are you up to date?

- Every state can have their own regulations and taxes. As well as legislation that protects consumers or that influences the trading or service environment.

  Business bills can be introduced without your knowledge and you or your team of professionals have to be aware of any regulatory changes that might require additional investments, payments, or simply vary your operation. A great way to stay on top of these types of changes is to be well advised by people who know, from your accountant, to your local chamber of commerce or business association. Be involved and up to date it will always present you with the information needed to stay on top of your game.

7. Is your business designed for your own wellbeing?

- Does your business strategy include a work – life balance?

  Managing your own business will require a lot of effort, a lot of time. And your enthusiasm and resilience will be tested! That is almost certain if you don't achieve the necessary work – life balance that includes your family and friends.

- This must form part of your strategy, from the beginning. Not only for yourself, but for your employees.

- Whatever goals you set, or whatever plans you are executing, you MUST include this in your goals to aim for. Set time for yourself, unwind from time to time.

And remember, no amount of success is worth anything

If you have no one to share and enjoy it with.

CHAPTER 2
Knowing and Building the right team:

Ok, so you have a great idea, your market research and the funds needed to start are ready! There are a lot of factors involved in getting a startup operating, or building and managing a successful company. And one of the most important factors will be the people you surround yourself with.

That alone, can determine the success or failure of your company. And even though there is no perfect formula, here are some tips that guide you in the hiring process so you can find the best possible team to help you achieve your goals.

- What are the important areas in a business and who should form part of the team?

A. Accounting:

Depending on several factors of your business strategy, the accounting team will play an important role in having healthy finances and knowing your options when considering a loan, growth or the areas that can be improved.

This area has to count with the right team from the beginning. Considering it is a specialized field and highly regulated, you can either hire a professional to handle your finances in house. Or you can evaluate an accounting firm that suits your business size. In BOTH cases you need to interview them to establish if they have the necessary experience and knowledge to help your business.

Options:

You can outsource a good bookkeeper to handle your day to day operations.

There are payroll companies that handle paychecks and you can talk to your bank for assistance or guidance in this matter.

You can hire a CPA for Tax accounting.

Be aware when evaluating qualifications in the accounting services areas. You can find persons who know finances, numbers, and the software required to manage adequately your financial information. And that sounds great, but, if they DO NOT KNOW your business or are NOT INTERESTED in learning your business, that might be very harmful. Either a company you hire, or a person, you have to be sure that they will not only do it properly, but that they will be willing to teach you, guide you, and assist you in finding options to improve your operation, reduce o manage costs, or maintain finances healthy.

A person or company responsible for your accounting or Finances has to be able to provide you with the information needed to take action and make decisions regarding your business.

Some of the tasks that need to be covered by this area include:

- Bank Balances

- Daily Summary of Sales

- Accounts receivable

- Accounts Payable

- Taxes

- Payroll

- Profit and Loss Statements

- Balance Sheets

B. Sales Team:

You will lead the sales team when you are in your initial stage of operations. It does not matter what type of business, if it is a restaurant, veterinary clinic, architecture firm, technology company, whatever your company does, you will lead the sales process. It will depend on your abilities, knowledge and desire, how much you sell, how often you sell it and if your costumers are satisfied.

Regardless of who knocks on the client's door, or who serves them, or who visits them. You started this project, what you define as the strategy, will either lead the company to success, or define the changes needed to adapt and grow.

If you are the initial sales representative of the company, be sure you measure your effectiveness. Be on top of your timelines, sales cycle and results. Why? Because if you grow and hire new reps, you want them to be as good, if not better than you.

For example

Case 1:

If you are a new restaurant owner, you will want to tend tables, interact with your customers, and evaluate how long it takes for plates to come out. At the same time be on top of the quality of the food, the costumer's experience. All of this you must know it by heart so you can demand quality service when you hire someone to represent you in front of costumers. The new servers will be a key part on how long the costumers stay in the restaurant, if they order more, if they are satisfied and more importantly, if they return. In this case, food is your product, the service level would represent your sales process. You have to know it to hire the right people.

If you are going to analyze your operation, you will find out that every employee within your restaurant will play part of your sales process. Each of them will contribute a portion of your service, or product. And it is important that you know all the roles. And if you can do all of them for a week, and see their perspective so you can find out what you can change or improve.

Case 2:

You are a Technology Company and you developed a software that will help millions. You are a brilliant developer but have a hard time interacting with costumers, or convincing them on why they need to buy it.

You have never sold anything in your life. But when you interview your sales representative, you will realize a very important sale. You will sell your vision, your product and where you can make a difference.

The person you hire to represent not only you, but your vision. He can assist you in learning how to talk to costumers, get appointments and close deals.

Now consider, it could be the other way around, you could have an idea for a software solution, but have no clue how it works and you require technicians to visit clients and explain it, you know how to get the meetings, the players in the game and how to convince anyone to buy anything; they know computers, software, how it works. But do you think they will be able to explain it clearly to a financial manager? A general manager?

In sales, communication is key. And if you need the technical knowledge to sell a product, well the obvious answer is have the technical person present it and try to sell it. But the effectiveness of this can delay sales, or loose deals.

One of the strategies that best worked for me, was to do it as a team at the beginning. Going to meetings together, seeing how he interacts with potential customers, how he dresses, how he acts, manners, how well he knew the products, etc. This allowed me to see how the costumers reacted. And my position was to be the specialist. Answer the technical questions, solve inquiries about implementation, variations, solutions, details that the sales rep may not have known, but as he heard me, he learned to the point where his visits were more efficient. And instead of 4 or 5 meetings to close a deal, it took only 2 or 3.

*Establishing the sales process is key to measure success. **You will have to lead it from the front and directly with costumers, or have the ability to evaluate the results of your employees.***

When you interview Sales Representatives you want to consider:

- What experience do they have in your field?

- Do they know the market? How long have they been in the market?

- Can they list the top 5 competitors? (Local and National if possible) – Can they list their strengths and weaknesses?

- Can they describe their sales process? (How do they get the costumers, what happens in a presentation, how long does it usually take them to close the deal, how many meetings?)

- Give them a few moments to get to know your product or service, explain it to them clearly, and have them give a presentation to your team the next day.

- If they had to set sales goals for themselves, what would the goals be? In $, Units, or specific quantities? *This can give you an idea of what they can expect to achieve themselves. They can set the bar really high, and if in a short period you realize they will not achieve it, ask them why the variation on what he offered? It can let you learn about something that needs to change, in the process or in the team. And if he achieves it, well, awesome.

It is very important that you realize this in any area that you are hiring. FOCUS on hiring people who can learn from you and who can teach you.

C. Marketing and social Media

If you are a small company and do not have the resources to hire a marketing manager, or a social media manager, do not worry. There are options so you can form a team with little resources. And if you are a company that has a marketing manager or social media manager, well there are ideas that might help you reduce your costs.

Very similar to the sales representative, a marketing or social media employee has to know your company in every stage. They have to know your costumer, your sales process, what you offer, your level of service and your costumer's expectations.

If you need a marketing team, similar to accounting, there are the options of in house or outsourcing. There are companies that can assist you with creating campaigns, strategies, ad designs, etc.

If you are looking to hire a marketing company or employee for in house, the principles will be the same. How well do they know your business? Your product or service? Your market?

First of all, before you interview anyone, you need to learn that information, regarding your market. It is essential so you and the marketing employee or company are on the same page.

And at the same time, it will help you evaluate how well they know it and if they can really help you achieve success with a marketing strategy.

When you interview a person or company for social media or marketing, a very important aspect they need is the experience level they have reaching the people who YOU would like to reach.

Be careful with spectacular ads and ideas that will become a major expense if directed to the wrong people. There are people and companies who are very creative and can develop a spectacular campaign, and advertising strategy. But if they do not know your business and costumer, they can make you spend a lot of money without any tangible results.

A lot of marketing companies and employees will try and measure success with the number of likes, in a page, the number of fans, and the level of digital interaction they create. That is worth little if it doesn't bring costumers through your doors or orders.

Most people confuse marketing and social media with advertising. Creating a visual campaign that will make your current and potential costumers identify your company, its products or services. And they would be correct, but actually no. Marketing and social media are based on the same principle, a communication channel with your current or potential costumer.

An ad is simply a visual representation of what your company can offer. You have to be clear that a marketing campaign is NOT JUST a series of ads running in newspapers, radio, TV, etc. In those cases, you are transmitting a message, but rarely can you quantify if the message was received and if it influenced a purchase decision. Those strategies are very hard to quantify.

If a marketing company or employee proposes this without getting to know your company or business, and just makes a nifty creative and awesome presentation, well, that is a BIG RED FLAG.

As a small business marketing can be a major investment, and that could put your company at risk if not handled properly. So the person or team you hire in house, or outsourced. They need to understand where you are and where you want to go. And they have to present you with viable options for your size, objectives and goals. And MORE IMPORTANTLY give you a strategy to reach and COMMUNICATE with the costumers you have and the ones you want to reach.

When seeking a person or a company to help you with your marketing and social media, you as the business owner need to know and create a strategy before hiring anyone to manage or execute it, from my experience, there are two types of strategies that you need to focus when developing a marketing strategy.

1. How to get current customers to be loyal and come back (Repeat business)

2. How to reach potential new customers that do not know your company (New Business)

BUILDING THE RIGHT TEAM

If your goal is to grow out of a one person operation, you have to be conscious that even the best business owner can only achieve so much. If you know your abilities, you have to be aware of your limitations, and the areas where you need a team to ensure your success.

After recognizing the areas where you lack expertise, or where you want to expand, you have to be able to recognize the individuals that will form part of a team that will lead your company to the next level.

A key part of this transition is to find the right people, and not only make them want to join you, but also who are willing to be led by you and are motivated by you. Any person that becomes part of your team has to integrate to what you want to achieve, and either follow your guide, or help you define how to reach the goals you have set for the company. And you, as the owner and leader, have to be able to motivate, and be motivated by them. They have to bring out the best in you, and you have to bring out the best in them.

IDENTIFY YOUR NEEDS – answer the following questions.

Is your business strategy defined?

Do you want to expand, open another office, store, location? If you have the strategy set and you are sure of exactly what you want to achieve, then it will be a lot easier to recognize where you will require specific skills and personnel to help you execute your business strategy.

Can you identify the skills required to grow and the areas of your business that are not performing well?

Are your finances healthy enough to apply for a business loan? Are your suppliers giving you the best options? Does your marketing strategy deliver results? Can you quantify those results? If you determine what area of your business is going to require more expertise, then you can identify the skills you need for the right employee to form part of your team. Can you specify the underperforming areas within your business? Usually if it is underperforming, you can re gain control with additional management skills.

Even if you have a lot of experience and expertise in many areas, you can be lacking the necessary skills to run every area efficiently. You may not be able to supervise every aspect of your business and if you try to handle too many responsibilities, you can be putting growth, development and even your own company at risk.

There are certain areas you may require assistance as you grow, it may be required for you to understand how they can benefit you. And speaking with a leader in that area might guide you to determine if it is needed or not in your company.

For example:

- Human resources

- IT

- Marketing (If you outsource and believe you want to create your own department)

- Sales Managers

- Territory Managers

- Financial Manager

- Legal

As you grow, not all areas within your company will grow at the same time or speed. There are criteria you have to meet to understand if you require additional personnel or services. But one thing is clear, every expansion, or new hire within your company, must have a purpose. If you hire more salespeople or a sales manager, you have to re adjust your goals, expenses and income accordingly. If you require HR personnel it can be to reduce employee turnover, or for trainings, etc. IT managers or employees to bring your processes into the latest technology and with the objective of becoming more efficient, saving money, saving time, improving customer service, etc. A financial manager has to present you with a clear financial plan that can guide your company to save on resources, or prepare for expansion, and will assist you in making the right decisions on investments, expenses, where to cut costs, etc.

The most important aspect of finding the right team for your company is to develop a well-managed and balanced team. That will appeal to future investors, clients, and anyone involved with your company and its future development.

CHAPTER 3
Be Specific about what you require from a new recruit

A very important aspect of hiring a new team member is to know exactly what you need them to offer your company. If you have previously identified the needs of your company, you must match them with an individual who can offer them from the start. If you require an individual to expand your network, hire someone who already has a proven track record with a lot of contacts and potential customers.

If you need multiple or special skills, seek individuals who may cover several requirements. This will allow you to delegate responsibility in the long run, and create a support system and a strong management team.

Seek people who thrive on learning and teaching. You want team members who can guide, motivate and teach personnel. But at the same time are open to learn from employees and the different roles within the company. You need people who can grow with your company.

Know the roles: if you need assistance in areas where there is not a lot of movement, considering hiring part time, or outsourcing. These types of hires are applicable in specific projects or tasks, and may only be required for a short period of time. You need to know each role and its requirements to determine if it is truly essential for your business strategy or if it will become an expense that cannot be justified.

Acquiring Options: Sometimes, a full time hiring is not needed to start, you can evaluate using freelance contractors, interns, students part time or asking a friend who is expert on the subject as a consultant if he can provide you with an idea of how he would cover the position.

You have to be able to financially and operationally justify talent acquisition. If you cannot hire for in house operation, seek outside assistance. And no matter if it is going to be inside or outside, be sure of EXACTLY what you need the position to do. When evaluating a position always ask yourself or your team if it could be done part time, or with a flexible schedule so you can have a more ample number of recruits and be able to keep costs to a minimum. There is always the option of training existing personnel with new skills so they can handle the requirements needed for a potential new position.

Working well with others: Once you grow, and the amount of people in your company increases, personalities will start to influence. The work environment, results, and a lot of aspects that can either help or harm your company.

To begin, you have to be aware and understand your personality, and how your employees will have to accept it and be able to with you. At the same time, every time you hire a new employee you have to be clear of who they will have to deal with and if they can handle - for example: customers, suppliers, employees, complaints, requests, etc.

Knowing an individual's personality before hiring them is not a simple task, but when you verify references, be sure to ask a person who worked directly with the individual to give you an idea. And also you can find tests with a professional, or after a bit of research online, that can guide you on a person's personality to help you with your decision.

As the leader of the company, your personality will reflect broadly on your personnel, but you also have to know that hiring people with difficult or conflicting personalities can create problems. If you are aware of your employees personality you can create healthy tension too, for example, managers who are not similar may help you see the difference in management styles and leadership. And you as the leader can learn. Additionally, if personnel have very similar personalities, they can dislike and neglect the same aspects of the business and limit your opportunities to improve.

How to find potential employees

After evaluating all your requirements, skills, personality and every aspect needed for the position you have to find suitable candidates.

- o The first place to look for adequate personnel is within your own network. You might already know strong job candidates from your past work experience, or with family and friends. Evaluate all your past working relationships, include customers, suppliers, competitors and other businesses that can present you with options or referrals.
- o Local newspaper advertising can be an option to make your offer reach more potential candidates, this however, requires you to

filter every application, and if you lack experience in doing so, you can invest a lot of time in reducing the pool of candidates.

- o If you have the option of utilizing a recruiting agency, it may allow you to find persons with the skills you need and it will be the recruiting agency's job to filter out the best candidates for your company. For this option, you have to consider the additional cost and if it is justified.
- o Internet sites that specialize in recruitment have a great source of candidates, you can seek that option but it will be similar to advertising. You will have to figure out and filter all suitable and potential employees.
- o If your company utilizes social media, you can post in sites like LinkedIn, twitter, Facebook and any other that allows you to drive potential employees to your website so they can review the opportunities you currently have open.
- o If your company has partners, investors or have a relationship with consultants, those people might present you with viable options for candidates.

Filtering down your potential candidates

Once you have identified all suitable prospects, you have to prepare yourself to evaluating their abilities, experience, knowledge and what they can do for your company.

As previously stated, it is critical you have a list of exactly what you require for the new position. This includes your expectations, your needs as the owner, what they are expected to do, and how they are expected to do it.

When preparing yourself for an interview you have to take into consideration the following:

- Before you set up the interview you need to revise his qualifications and verify the references. If the applicant can provide a resume and add a cover letter to explain why he would benefit the company. It would be ideal.

- Be clear about what you require for the position. All the responsibilities that are involved in performing the job and you and your company's expectations.

- Once you initiate the interview, try to assess the candidate's personality, try to figure out if they have the right mindset, qualities by role playing if possible, try to determine how they would react with specific situations that are important for the position.

- Small business owners often require candidates to be self-motivated, who can work independently or with little to no supervision, this type of trait is not easy to find just in an interview, you will require to test out his motivation and skills to make sure he can fulfill the requirements. A characteristic of a person who likes to work independently and with little supervision is that they have a hard time following orders or being supervised. Be clear that they do not get that confused, that the position requires constant feedback and reporting, and if they do it in an efficient and organized manner is critical to the performance of the position.

- When interviewing, use open questions where they can explain situations in specific scenarios, or where you might need a skill evaluated. "Can you tell me your worst experience with a costumer?" / listen to the answer and see if they only share an anecdote or if they present how they solved it and handled it too.

- You need to be sure that they understand the role and requirements, for this you can ask them if they could explain what their role and priorities should be.

- If the person being considered for a position is appealing to your company, and they will become part of a team, ask a team member to interview them. Someone who will work with them directly. That additional opinion can give you a perspective you did not consider, and might help you determine other factors to take in account when deciding to hire a new employee.

- For the right candidate to be happy starting a new job, they have to believe in the business. This is one of the cases where the business plan will assist you in guiding your employees. They have to believe in what they are going to do, you have to be credible in what you offer, and how it will be achieved. You have to sell your company and vision to the potential employee, but DO NOT offer things you are not sure if you will be able to provide.

- You have to convince them in the opportunity, not only the financial aspects of the position, but the change and experiences you offer. Make them understand that their performance can influence the growth of the company and make a difference.

- Take your time. Do not hire in the moment. Evaluate all the candidates you can and once you have found suitable candidates, take MORE time. You need to be certain of the individual, because for a small company, every hire is a critical step in the right or wrong direction.

Why is hiring the right people so important

- As part of the interview process, try to determine the plans and dreams they have in the short term, midterm and if possible long term. Any position, for any company can be a risk if the person hired is just there in the meanwhile. As soon as something better comes along, they will leave without hesitation. If they are money oriented, that is a consideration to take when making a decision to hire someone. Big companies can afford to replace employees without affecting the company. But small businesses have trouble finding right candidates, and keeping them. That can cause an unstable environment for the rest of employees and overall work moral may be affected.

- You want an individual who can become part of your plans, propose them, help them execute them and love your company as much as you do. That depends specifically on how you present your company, the position and if you are credible.

- Having a plan is critical to finding the right employees; and for a small company, it is even more important when hiring. You cannot afford to lose personnel every couple of months and re invest in training, and everything that involves a position in your company.

- If sales reps leave, then the relationship with your clients might be in jeopardy. Did you retain them or will they take them and you lost the business?

- If the service staff of your restaurant leaves often and you can't keep them, will your client service suffer? Off course. Will the clients notice different personnel every time they arrive? That can influence a lot in the food service industry.

- If a manager is not properly hired, and has access to sensitive information, and after just one year he decides to leave. Could that pose a risk? Could he take sensitive information, or more importantly, other team members and employees?

Once you have decided who the best candidate for the position is, present the new employee with a formal written proposal that details his financial conditions, schedules, responsibilities, tasks, and all his legal details for employment information.

With this presented and signed by both parties you can now present an introduction to the team and the induction program to your operation. Once the employee initiates the job, make sure he follows a plan that allows him to get up to speed in the operation and how he can contribute to the business.

For management positions you have to prepare all the necessary information for his job to be done properly, that includes the information relevant to his position in the business plan, the account information he will have to manage and the policies and procedures that are key for the company's success.

Motivating a team – the right leadership

- As the owner of a small business you have to understand that all the different positions within the company can vary on factors that drive the employees. Because of this, you need to be aware of what motivates each of your team members.

- Each position within your company will vary in degree of responsibility, you as the leader and owner have to be clear on what are the priorities for each employee and the goals they have to achieve in order to reach the objectives set in your business plan. Not only do you have to be clear yourself with each position and employee, but more importantly, you have to communicate it clearly so they understand what is expected from them and the importance they play in your company's success.

- *When determining the levels of responsibility for each employee, make sure you are able to share and delegate the responsibility.* As a small business owner you often want to be involved and on top of everything. And this is possible to a certain point, but if your goal is to grow and become more efficient, you have to trust your employees and their skills. And this will obligate you to DELAGATE certain aspects of the operation where you usually took care of things and now might not need to invest a lot of time for it to get done.

- *Make sure your senior and key employees are involved in important decisions.* They can help you make difficult choices a bit easier and the can present you with options on how to achieve the goals required for your company. If you delegate and trust your employees, you need to give them the freedom required to complete their tasks and fulfill their responsibilities. But make sure you are always available if they need your support, and make it clear to them that your role as owner is to help them when needed. But make SURE you do not fall in the micro manager role in their activities, this can create a burden for them and for you.

- *Communication is the key for a successful company.* As a business owner you have to make difficult choices often, and without the adequate information, that becomes a risk factor for your company. This is why communication is a key aspect in the performance of your business. As you understand this you have to implement the communication channels from the top to the bottom. You have to encourage your employees to share concerns, listen carefully to opinions and when feedback is provided.

Once you have the necessary information, you have to ACT on the issues that have been raised. An important factor in employee morale is when they feel they are not listened to, or that their opinion does not matter, so pay attention and when you offer to make a change, deliver. If it is not possible to make a change, make sure you explain it clearly to the employee. And keeping them in the loop will always make them feel important.

- Hold scheduled performance reviews. Establish a calendar for yourself and your management team where you evaluate your team's performance. Use these evaluations as the opportunity to discuss any concerns that might arise.

Depending on the size of the company, this might be a simple task or a time consuming task, but you have to determine the importance of it. Not only to verify if your communication is effective with your managers, but also to evaluate if low level employees are being heard by their own managers. All the levels of communication have to be efficient for the company to be able to adapt to change and avoid problems that might arise internally.

- *Growth opportunities.* When a team member has reached a peak within the operation, they might feel tempted to seek other opportunities, and that will happen with or without your company. They might have gained enough experience for a new position, or more responsibilities. If your communication is effective, and there is trust, an employee will reach out to you first. And especially if there is a culture of growth in your company.

To avoid or minimize employees to seek opportunities elsewhere, you need to consider training or development programs and activities that can benefit the employee and your company. If you have employees that are interested in trying out different roles or assuming more responsibility, create the chance and be honest with them if the opportunity can be handled in house or if you require an external employee with a different level of skills or experience.

If you can provide the training or courses needed for them to acquire the skills and experience and it is a viable option for your company, then promote that. But only invest in personnel that can make a commitment to your company. If you offer training they have to work a minimum of time in your company so the investment in training makes sense for both.

- Positive Feedback to Employees. When an employee is loyal, hardworking, and gets the results you require from them, it is important to recognize it from time to time. There are special people who go above the call of duty, and most of them do not do it for the recognition. It is because they truly enjoy and believe in what they do. And if time goes by and they do not feel appreciated, that might put their continuity at risk.

Identify the individuals who are successful and recognize their contribution to your company. And find a way to make them feel special and appreciated. It may be with the team to try and motivate others, or it might be privately to make sure they understand and are aware that YOU recognize their hard work. A simple great job, and thank you for your effort can provide the inspiration needed to continue that behavior. And you as the leader have to be able to recognize, appreciate and value such actions.

- Employee Incentives. When you are able to track and evaluate your employee's performance in an efficient and careful manner, you can establish a set of pre-arranged targets to motivate employees if they achieve such targets. This can be integrated to a performance based incentive pay strategy, but be careful on how you plan it.

If you do not have the experience in creating one, you have to evaluate it carefully or consult with someone who has the knowledge to structure one that will not affect your business financially speaking. When companies need to increase sales they develop such programs to try and motivate a team, but if you do not consider all the financial aspects, it can become a risk and create a results obsessed culture in the company.

If you want to motivate a team, but are unsure of how to do it, you can surprise them with a small bonus, a gift certificate, or an incentive they might find attractive. If you have clear goals and objectives, you can individually track performance and reward if met. You set your goals, communicate it to the team and if it is achieved, then provide an incentive. It can range from a financial incentive, to an extra day or afternoon off, or a dinner, movie tickets or anything that is suitable to your current capabilities.

DO NOT start an incentive program if it is something your will offer but cannot deliver. Many times companies develop a program that has loopholes and at the end do not deliver what was presented to employees. Be aware that you can structure it to individuals, or a certain position within your company, but you have to realize that there is a team behind them. And if goals are met, everyone deserves a degree of recognition. If your sales reps reach goals and have monetary incentives, do the assistants in the office who handle the sales paperwork get incentives? Do the warehouse and drivers who deliver the products on time and keep the sales reps commitments get the recognition they deserve?

If you provide only managers with incentive programs it might make them change their behavior with employees just because they want to reach goals. That can cause the work environment to change and people to become frustrated with certain attitudes.

Individual incentives can be efficient, but you have to be aware of the people involved and recognize the achievements as a team.

Discuss it with your partners, loved ones or people who your trust or know the topic. And evaluate your financial aspect from the beginning. Run simulations of what it will cost you, who is involved and what you can reach if you put it in action. Monetary compensation for incentive is not always the answer, but it can be part of a great benefit if it is fair and makes sense for the entire company and all the members involved.

If you want to evaluate a compensation package then you can start by the specific goal you set. For example: I need to sell this X product or service more.

First consider: What is the profit margin on product or service X? If I put it on sale will that margin decrease? Is it always available, do I have the necessary stock? How many units do I want to sell? How many costumers actually buy it?

Once you have answered the previous question you can now determine the following: Who is involved in the sale of product X? How many sales reps promote it? Do they have assistants? Is there a manager involved? Is there warehouse or delivery personnel involved?

If the goal of selling more units of X product or service is reached, how much additional income will I generate? What percentage of that additional income can I distribute with everyone involved? How do I distribute that fairly? Do I pay in money or in something else? Like a certificate, gift, trip, TV, dinner, etc.?

Can I do this on a monthly basis? Do I do it every 3 or 6 months? Once a year?

There are several factors to consider when developing an incentives plan, you know your company and your employees, make sure to cover and analyze all bases so it doesn't become a risk instead of a reward that makes your team focus on short term performance or a specific task that makes them less interested in other responsibilities.

LEAD BY EXAMPLE

Being a business owner can be very stressful. Motivation can vary from time to time and make you change your behavior. This can influence your inspiration, creativity, desire and overall happiness. And if you lead a team. **Your actions speak louder than words.** Keeping yourself motivated and strong is easy in the good times, but when adversity is met on a daily basis, or when doubt knocks on your door, it is very difficult to keep your spirits up and set a good example for your employees. And don't get me wrong, this is something that might be caused in the hard times AND IN THE GOOD TIMES. If your business is doing very well, or not so well, it can influence in the same manner to helping you become a BAD example for your employees.

Going through a rough time scenario:

Money is tight, you are barely paying your expenses, your monthly income as an owner should be stable, but it is not. You have a tough time making payroll and are on complicated terms with suppliers. This scenario is a common situation on a daily basis for many business owners. And to be honest, some make it out of this, and some don't.

The toll this can have on your motivation is huge, the going to bed thinking and over analyzing what to do, how to fix it, where to get money, that is a burden you decided to carry the day you became a business owner. In the good times and in the bad times. And this affects not only you, but every employee in your company. Your attitude, your dedication. Your willingness to accept ideas, opinions, complaints, and everything that happens in your company. You arrive late, are always tired, you leave early, you don't communicate with employees, and you are overwhelmed.

It does not matter what led you to this situation, your attitude will define if you are able to overcome it or not. As a leader you make choices that can bring your success, or difficult lessons. And if those choices or circumstances affect the way you treat people, you yell at people, you are disrespectful or simply become uninterested, then you lack the leadership needed to run a successful company.

Your attitude is critical especially when you are going through a rough time. Your dedication and interest in succeeding has to be a key element on how you react to adversity. Never lose perspective of why you started the business, inspire your employees and make them believe in you. You are a leader and how you act with others will be important if you want to turn things around.

If your attitude and leadership are tested, be conscious that is what a small business owner will face, and there are solutions for everything, but if you set a bad example for your employees, it will reflect in every aspect of your business. Not answering calls from collectors, not wanting to talk to anyone, leaving early, arriving late, always being busy and not having time to even talk to your employees and hearing their concerns. Making excuses, not assuming responsibility, these are characteristics of a bad leader, and believe me, if you have gone through a hard time in your business, you will be tested, and your actions will define if you were meant to lead or to follow.

Doing great scenario:

Your company is thriving, you are happy and successful. Every business owner wants to achieve that from day one. And the time it takes to achieve it depends on so many factors that once you do. You may lose sight of what it took to get there.

There are so many companies that are in a generational transition, the parents started the business years ago, worked very hard to run a successful business and grow, and they achieved it. And now the new generation of owners come into place to manage an already started and successful business. It is what everyone wants to achieve, for them and for their family.

But here comes the tricky part. If you run a successful business, which you started, inherited, bought or whatever the scenario is, but you are the leader; then it gets to a point where it can become easy to lose sight of what it takes to keep it running successfully or taking the next step for growth.

The company already has a team that works efficiently, and the results are being delivered. You are not essential anymore for the business to operate on a daily basis. And this causes you to develop interest in something else, a hobby, another project, or simply start enjoying life and your success.

Every small business owner wants that. But many small business owners relate the income the company generates, with the success it has and how much it needs from their leadership. The company makes a lot of money, I have a great team, now I can start doing and enjoying myself.

But that is not necessarily the case every time. Sometimes business owners jump the gun. They are so happy that they generate the necessary income to live a comfortable life and start wandering, seeking other ventures, not paying enough attention to the business and not controlling personnel, supervising, etc. After all the hard work they are entitled, but if not careful, this behavior can lead to putting the company at risk.

Once you are successful, and generate enough income, then I do not need to show up every day. I am the owner and I have employees to do everything for me. So I can go golfing, partying, starting other projects without worrying of what will happen. I will receive the reports at the end of the week and see how much we made. And if there is any concern, I will call my managers and solve any doubts.

This behavior, if noticed by employees as the leader not being interested anymore, can put the company at risk.

Be aware of your attitude, and be conscious of how you lead others. Remember you have to earn the respect and trust of your employees. They have to believe in you and your ability to lead them. When you own the company, your actions and words have to match.

LEAD BY EXAMPLE TIPS

- Get to know your employees as much as you can.

- Never ask anyone (Client, supplier, employee) to do something you would not be willing to do.

- Be conscious of your moral and ethical compass. As well as your employees. If someone does not have the same values and principles, it may affect your business.

- Be clear with employees and customers about the standards of service you expect to deliver. And follow up to make sure it is being accomplished.

- Personally get involved with key customers and suppliers.

- NEVER offer something you are not sure you can deliver. Your word means a lot when you are a leader.

- If a problem or situation requires your attention, always be ready to help out.

- Be on time, to EVERYTHING. Appointments, meetings, calls, everything you commit yourself of doing at an expected time. That shows respect for your employees, clients and will define that you expect the same.

- First one in, and last one out of the office for as long as it takes to inspire others. Once you do, keep at it and show appreciation for people who give more than what is asked from them.

- Be honest with your employees, customers, suppliers and anyone that is involved in your business.

- NEVER EVER lie. If you do, you are enabling a culture of liars within your business.

- Be respectful, NEVER yell at employees or disrespect them. If your experience tells you that is the only way to make people understand. Well you are wrong, being disrespectful will do a lot more harm than good to a company. And a great leader will never need to make other's feel inadequate or disrespected to accomplish something or prove a point. If that is your personality, you need to seek professional help to change it. Believe me, at the end you will see the difference in the results.

-

It is not relevant if you already own and operate your business, or if you are in the planning stages to start it. The previous information can help you become aware of areas where you can be more conscious about your actions, or where you can become a better version of the leader you are. Be honest with yourself. Accept your shortcomings and make an effort to improve or change. It will make a difference.

Getting to know your Team and their roles:

Knowing each of your company positions, their responsibilities and tasks is an essential part to setting goals, evaluating performance, communicating and creating a strategy that allows your business to succeed.

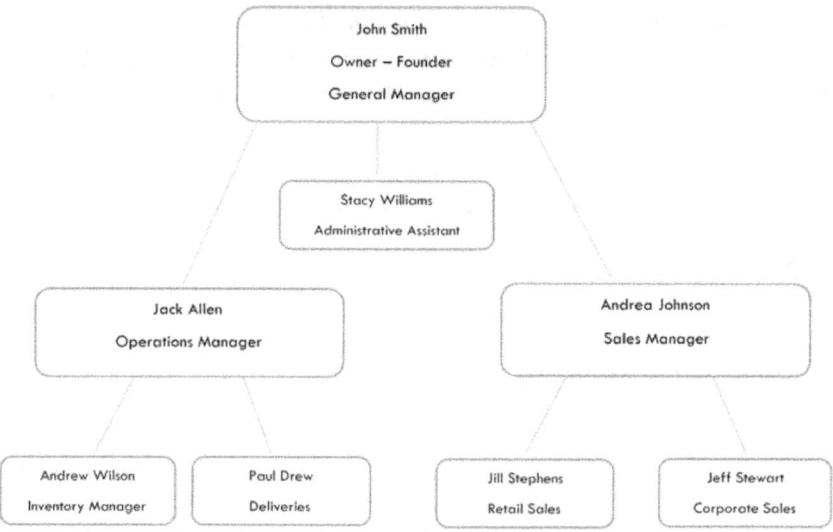

This represents a simple organizational chart of a company, or a simulation of the people you will require to start operating.

This allows you to visualize who is part of your team, Their level of responsibility within the company, what area are they involved with and who do they report to, or who reports to them.

After you create your own, we will go into detail to get an idea of each position, what it requires and the responsibilities they have.

Example of Excel sheet profile controls (Employee descriptions)

EMPLOYEE PROFILE - FINANCIAL - DEPARTMENT - TASKS

Department	Position	Employee	Base Salary	Travel Allowance	Gas	Commissions/ Bonus
				Monthly expense		
Management	General Manager	John Smith	$ 4,000.00	$ -	$ -	1% of bonus if monthly sales goals are surpassed.
Management	Administrative Assist	Stacy Williams	$ 2,500.00	$ -	$ -	none
Operations	Operations Manager	Jack Allen	$ 3,000.00	$ -	$ 500.00	none
Operations	Inventory Manager	Andrew Wilson	$ 2,500.00	$ -		none
Operations	Deliveries	Paul Drew	$ 2,500.00	$ -	varies	none
Sales	Sales Manager	Andrea Johnson	$ 3,000.00	variable	$ 500.00	2% of commission if sales quota is met
Sales	Retail Sales	Jill Stephens	$ 2,000.00	variable	$ 500.00	1% of commission if sales quota is met
Sales	Corporate Sales	Jeff Stewart	$ 2,000.00	variable	$ 500.00	1% of commission if sales quota is met

EMPLOYEE PROFILE - FINANCIAL - DEPARTMENT - TASKS

Department	Position	Employee	Monthly	Weekly	Daily
			Reports Due		
Management	General Manager	John Smith			
Management	Administrative Assist	Stacy Williams			
Operations	Operations Manager	Jack Allen	Purchases/ Deliveries/Inventory	Inventory	Purchases/ Deliveries
Operations	Inventory Manager	Andrew Wilson		Purchase Requisitions	Low Inventory
Operations	Deliveries	Paul Drew	Gas Report/Deliveries/Client report	Deliveries Made/client requisitions or comments.	Product Delivered
Sales	Sales Manager	Andrea Johnson			
Sales	Retail Sales	Jill Stephens			
Sales	Corporate Sales	Jeff Stewart			

Your employee profile and positions

The objective of the following exercise is to create a profile for each employee or position in your company.

Employee Name:
Position: Department:
Yearly Salary:
This position reports directly to:
Employees that report to this position:
Position Objectives: Describe the main objective of this position and the role it plays in your company's success.

Please list the following: Detail all the activities the position has to realize relevant to their position and objectives. List the ones that apply.

Daily Tasks
Weekly Tasks
Monthly Tasks:

Does this position have to issue reports: If the position requires to create, supervise, analyze or present reports, please indicate the type of report, the frequency, who it is addressed to and the objective.
Position Goals: If this position is structure with measurable goals please detail what they are and how they need to be achieved.
Skills and Personality: What do you require in personality traits for this position? What skills do the need to perform their duties?

Performance Indicators: what variables do you evaluate in the position to track performance? (Example, number of clients attended, sales figures, visits realized, effective visits that ended in sales, timelines for projects, etc.)

Each position you create a profile for will enable you to understand their needs, requirements and help you measure their performance. Additionally, you can add any information regarding the position, and at the same time help you when you need to hire a new employee for the position or replace an existing one.

CHAPTER 4

The Importance of Accurate Information

What type of information drives your business? As you may know by now, information is power. And currently we live in a world that is driven by the access that we have to any type of data we desire. It is available at your fingertips, and with it you can learn, verify and keep yourself entertained in almost any topic you desire.

Has this helped your business? Do you have a software system or the necessary skills to generate useful information to manage your company and make the right calls?

If you are currently just relying on your instincts and knowledge of the business, well, let me ask you a couple of questions:

- What drives your business decisions?

- What type of information do you analyze or have when considering expansions or changes in your business operation?

- What do you base on when hiring or firing employees?

- What comparison or evaluation do you realize when considering change of location?

- How do you track employee productivity?

With all the tools available now a days, companies should have no trouble accessing and analyzing the information they require to make decisions that benefit their success. But somehow, small business owners and people in general, are known for taking guesses or going with their gut feeling. And if you are one of them and are already operating small business, well trust me, you are not alone.

We have to understand that many starting business owners are pretty much relying on their instincts and knowledge to establish and grow a company. And there is nothing wrong with this, there are learning curves in every company; that allow you to gain the necessary experience to determine what type of information will be critical in assisting you to make better decisions.

You may be very organized, have an established business plan, a net and detailed budget and you are ready in any aspect possible.

But what happens if nothing goes as planned? Or if something varies from your initial or established strategy? You may be forced to take educated or logical guesses at those times, and that might help you come up with solutions or options.

When this type of reality strikes you, many are not prepared to adapt. You can have a plan but if you are not able to track progress close enough to react, a small bump in a strategy or a wrong turn can completely ruin your plans and put your company at risk.

You can justify any type of strategy or you can say it is part of the plan, to implement a software solution that will provide me with all the information I want or need. You can say "I cannot control all the information without software, or the technical skills, or I am not good at financial analysis. "

Every small business has the need to analyze and track results, if you do not have a software system that can give you all the data, you don't actually need one to gather useful information to track your progress and evaluate your results.

On the other hand, let's say you already have a software system that can do all of this for you. And you swear by it and trust everything it says, when you are low on inventory, when your sales are up or down, of whatever report the out of the box software solution provides you.

Let me make something clear, every software solution is based on pretty much the same design. Accounting, inventory, payroll, operations, sales, and maybe other modules that you find useful for your business. And they are important tools that will help you be organized and efficient in many aspects.

But it does not matter if you have or do not have a software solution. If you are not analyzing the information your business generates, or if you are not sure of the information you currently feed the software, then you are not prepared for change. If something is going on, or something happens and you need to react, if you are ill informed you will make ill decisions.

If you trust your sales reps because they know what they are talking about, and what they say is what goes when it comes to what you purchase, what sells and what your company should advertise, well my friend, you are headed to trouble town.

Most companies rely only on financial data, sales history, and simple global data that will help them repeat it every year if it is stable.

Let me present you an example of what I am trying to explain. In my research I reviewed an interesting article that can show you how important it is for you to consider the information you gather, how you analyze it and how it can benefit you.

I found an article in a blog that I find perfect to describe the importance of accurate Information.

The article read***:

"Think of a professional baseball team. Let's say that there is no ESPN or other statistical resource tracking specific data for us (since in the case of our businesses we are on our own). Instead, all we have is the standard Win/Loss record, total fan attendance, and individual player stats to base our management decisions on. At the end of a season, we need to make some big decisions: there are players up for free agency, others looking for contract extensions, we are considering some stadium enhancements, should we keep our coaching staff tact, what players should we try to trade, what type of positions do we need to fill, etc. (as a business owner, we face similar decisions)? Now, we won half of our games which was a ten-game improvement over last year, but attendance was down by an average of 20% per game, and we had the league MVP on our team with amazing stats but the other players were below league average stats-wise. So, do you think we're ready to make our business decisions now?

If you said yes, please contact me as I want to offer you a job. For the rest of us, we'd probably say something like "we need more data." In this example it might seem more obvious. Let's say we didn't have any more hard data but we did watch every game, spend time in the locker room, and feel pretty good in our gut what types of decisions we need to make. Feel better? This might give you more confidence but are you really more prepared? Most people feel they are prepared with this type of daily exposure to the business. However, let's evaluate some key components.

Why was attendance down even though our record was improved? If I was setting up a reporting system for attendance I would want to track attendance based on days of week, opposing teams, who was playing or pitching, weather conditions, division standings, national holidays, local event schedule, our Win/Loss record and games within playoff contention at various points in the season, and much more. Why is this type of detailed information important? Well, a pure number like attendance is only as good to me as this other relative data. The entire picture needs to be painted to really come up with data that can be used to determine our lack of success at the box office.

What about the decision to keep players, the coach, etc.? Are stats enough? Maybe in fantasy baseball they are enough but the actual game of Major League Baseball is not that simple."

(***Article from: http://www.thewebsitecenter.net/blog/item/81-reporting-the-importance-of-accurate-meaningful-data.html)

Big companies are complex, and small businesses too! Million or billion dollar companies started out as a small business. But just because your company is not a million or billion dollar company is it ok to rely on your instincts. One of the steps they took to get to where they are was to make well informed decisions. And you can start doing that; you cannot say "We're just a small company" to justify your lack of or not efficient decision making.

You, as the business owner, have to create the steps needed to collect and report data.

What information is useful for my company?

You need to start by determining the areas of your business that need to be tracked.

- What performance indicators do you require to make better and informed decisions?

- Which employees, processes or areas within your company do you need to track performance?

- Some important aspects of business intelligence can focus in areas like sales, inventory, time management, costs, expenses and costumer history.

- Do you have a software system that con provide it, and is it configured to provide you with the reports needed?

  - If you are unsure, you can inquire with the software supplier or someone familiar with it so they can provide you with the options you require.

  - If you need to train yourself or someone within your company to gather the knowledge experience of the system, that is an important step and you have to assume or assign the responsibility. If you as a business owner can be shown how to properly access and review it.

- If you do not have a history of information you can analyze, you have to start creating one. You need to start gathering the data.

- You as the business owner can establish the steps required and the people involved in the data gathering process. You can start requiring reports on their activities and input them into a simple excel sheet so you can create a pool of information that will help you evaluate performance and results.

- Once you have established the areas where you need monitoring you have to determine the frequency of evaluation. How often do you need to revise the information? Each area you deem important will provide you with performance indicators.

- The frequency of reporting and monitoring your data will determine how quickly you can react to any unforeseen circumstances in your operation.

  - Examples:

  - If you review inventory and purchase orders every couple of months, you can spend weeks without products. And that might result in a dip in sales and customer satisfaction.

  - If your sales team are not visiting as many costumers as previous months, you can miss opportunities to increase your sales. For instance, a sales rep just closed a big deal that pretty much covers his sales quota for the quarter. That sales rep can relax and not worry about additional sales because he already surpassed his goal. That means he can waste time and not visit frequent or potential customers because he doesn't need to.

- If you own a restaurant and revise the number of costumers a server tended to, but you don't compare it to other servers, you cannot know who is actually working hard and who is slacking.

- If you visit 10 potential costumers per month and are able to close 4 deals within that time period, and one of your reps visits 40 potential customers and closes 10 deals within the same time period, who is more effective?

- A key aspect of reports and what you should evaluate, there is a famous term that applies perfectly for this matter if you are starting out= KISS (Keep it Simple Stupid) if you get too much information and too many results you might not be able to focus on what is important. Remember, the more options you have, the more time it may take to make decisions. It depends on your ability to analyze and make decisions.

- When starting to gather data, do not go gathering ALL OF IT from the start. Try to determine 1 to 3 important areas within your business that will give you a detailed view of the performance in a specific process, department or employee. Start with the one you consider most important, and master it, get to know the numbers by heart and the history. Set a time period for evaluation, a couple of reports can determine if the information is critical or if you need to compliment it.

- As the owner and manager, you have to get the right information, so try to pinpoint the information you require to evaluate how your company and personnel are performing.

Besides the traditional financial reports issued by your accounting, sales and profits, balance sheets, etc. Try to add specific reports in specific departments or areas. DO NOT do everything at once, step by step is the key. *And remember KISS.*

If you start the data gathering and analysis process without a software, you might get to a point where you want a software to make that process easier. But remember, when seeking a software system you have to consider two important things:

- Seek a software that can adapt to your business processes or can clearly improve them.

  Never purchase a software if you don't understand it and its capabilities. And if you are unsure if you need to adapt to it, seek other options.

- Seek a software supplier that KNOWS about business processes. And even better if they have experience in your field. They have implemented a solution for a company similar to yours and you can verify it.

Why is this important?

When purchasing a software for small businesses, usually the company has done things their way for a long time, and it has worked, so business owners and employees can be scared or not willing to change. And if you decide to purchase a system that will make huge changes in your process, chances are that your employees will not use it properly and the data you receive from it will not be totally accurate. That is why it is very important that YOU as the business owner understand what information is important for you to manage the company. If you know exactly what you need, you can ask the company based on the reports you require, to present you a solution. A simple "These are the reports I need every week, there are monthly, and these are quarterly" can you software deliver them?

Daily Sales Example:

As you can see in the picture below, I created an excel sheet with all the days of the month. Each tab represents a day of the month. On each tab, I gather the information from each customer, what they bought and contact information.

No.	Costumer	Pet	Dr.	Assistant	Service	Invoice No.	Payment Method	SubTotal	Total	TEL	Record	New or Return	EMAIL
1	RITA DE HERNANDEZ	BARRY	MOR	JOSUE	TX	6632	CASH	$ 150.00		59024705	936	RE	ritadhernandez@hotmail.com
					HOSPITALIZACION	6632	CASH	$ 161.00		59024705	936	RE	ritadhernandez@hotmail.com
					RX	6632	CASH	$ 189.00	$ 500.00	59024705	936	RE	ritadhernandez@hotmail.com
2	ILEANA CHAVARRIA	COCO	FERMIN	RENE	RX	6633	CASH	$ 172.00		52018370	198	RE	mangel_1963@hotmail.com
					CONSULTA	6633	CASH	$ 135.00	$ 307.00	52018370	198	RE	mangel_1963@hotmail.com
3	IRMA YOLANDA BARILLAS LARA	FIONA	FER	GUST	TX	6630	CASH	$ 150.00				NEW	
					RECARGO	6630	CASH	$ 75.00	$ 225.00	24719624	2713	RE	mimi.55yd@gmail.com
4	MIRCY BARRIOS	JESSIE	LUIS	JOSUE	TX	6634	CASH		$ 142.00		629	RE	no tiene
5	GLORIA DE VILLATORO	SAM			BCU	6635	CC	$ 125.00					
		VICEN			BCU	6635	CC	$ 125.00	$ 250.00		554	RE	NO TIENE
6	DENNILSON MAZUL	CHARLY	LUIS		LAB	6636	CC	$ 380.00					
					ultrasondio	6636	CC	$ 350.00	$ 730.00	45770376	1919	RE	mazul999@hotmail.com
7	JEANETTE MORALES	PEQUE			BAÑO	6637	CASH		$ 50.00		2069	RE	no tiene
8	diego armando coton	NEGRITA			TX	6638	CC		$ 142.00		2714	RE	diegocoton27@gmail.com
9	MARIANA CABRERA	BLACKY	LUIS		MULTIPLE	6639	CASH		$ 198.00	30015101	2615	NEW	no tiene
10	MARCO VINICIO GIRON	JACK			BAÑO	6640	CASH		$ 60.00	24417623	1669	RE	yanjarag@yahoo.com
11	MIGUEL DE LEON	DAYSI	LUIS	JOSUE	TX	6641	CC		$ 142.00		617	RE	donmigue@hotmail.com
12	RITA CASTILLO	FRUO			TX		CC		$ 142.00				

(Figure a – Client Data in Daily Sales)

At the end of the day, I added up all my income.

No.	Costumer	Pet	Dr.	Assistant	Service	Innvoice No.	Payment Method	SubTotal	Total
50									
									$ 2,888.00
	Cash	$ 1,102.49			Number of Clients	12			
	Check								
	CC (Credit Card)	$ 1,406.00							
	On Credit								
	Purchases	$ 379.51							
	TOTAL	$ 2,888.00	DIF:	-					
	Purchases								
	DESCRIPTION	AMOUNT							
1	sueros	$ 43.30							
2	laboratorios	$ 247.00							
3	cadenas	$ 89.21							
4									
15									
		$ 379.51							

As you can see, at the bottom of the daily sales, I added up the income, how they paid, and the number of clients we had that day. As well as listed all the purchases from petty cash. (Including a description of what we bought)

What can be done with this information? If I repeat this process every day, I can create a monthly report of income and expenses. And with the monthly report I can control what came into the company, if I provided credit to any special clients, and the daily purchase amounts to control my expenses.

Each line added up my totals from the daily sales, and at the end of the month I had all the information regarding my daily operation. (Financially speaking off course).

MONTHLY REPORT

DATE	CASH	CHECKS	CREDIT CARD	ON CREDIT	PURCHASES	TOTAL	Number of Clients
1	$ -	$ -	$ 250.00	$ -	$ -	$ 250.00	1
2	$ 904.49	$ -	$ 1,156.00	$ -	$ 379.51	$ 2,440.00	12
3	$ 1,102.49	$ -	$ 1,406.00	$ -	$ 379.51	$ 2,888.00	12
4	$ 1,102.49	$ -	$ 1,406.00	$ -	$ 379.51	$ 2,888.00	12
5	$ 1,264.00	$ -	$ 379.51	$ 2,746.00	$ -	$ 4,389.51	15
6	$ -	$ 1,102.49	$ -	$ 1,264.00	$ -	$ 2,366.49	11
7	$ 994.50	$ 590.00	$ 563.00	$ 1,621.00	$ 226.50	$ 3,995.00	14
8	$ 1,499.70	$ -	$ 625.00	$ 235.00	$ 856.30	$ 3,216.00	7
9	$ 2,711.00	$ -	$ 588.00	$ 72.00	$ 688.00	$ 4,059.00	14
10	$ 619.00	$ -	$ 911.00	$ 50.00	$ 207.00	$ 1,787.00	8
11	$ -	$ -	$ -	$ -	$ -	$ -	
12	$ 71.00	$ 1,682.00	$ 4,585.00	$ 610.00	$ 912.00	$ 7,860.00	21
13	$ 169.00	$ 727.00	$ 585.00	$ -	$ 408.00	$ 1,889.00	6
14	$ 679.00	$ 1,738.00	$ 2,310.00	$ 300.00	$ 393.00	$ 5,420.00	13
15	$ 565.00	$ 1,379.00	$ 3,129.00	$ -	$ 31.00	$ 5,104.00	14
16	$ 421.50	$ 200.00	$ 1,917.00	$ 802.00	$ 366.50	$ 3,707.00	10
17	$ 641.00	$ 1,250.00	$ 2,587.00	$ -	$ 265.00	$ 4,743.00	12
18	$ -	$ -	$ -	$ -	$ -	$ -	
19	$ 200.00	$ 1,951.00	$ 1,076.00	$ -	$ -	$ 3,227.00	11
20	$ 980.00	$ 331.00	$ 651.00	$ -	$ 50.00	$ 2,012.00	8
21	$ 503.50	$ 2,000.00	$ 535.00	$ 142.00	$ 106.50	$ 3,287.00	13
22	$ 1,011.10	$ -	$ 410.00	$ -	$ 29.90	$ 1,451.00	7
23	$ 2,190.00	$ 257.00	$ 155.00	$ 196.00	$ 15.00	$ 2,813.00	9
24	$ 498.00	$ 248.00	$ 2,267.00	$ -	$ 185.00	$ 3,198.00	11
25	$ -	$ -	$ -	$ -	$ -	$ -	
26	$ 826.50	$ 4,300.00	$ 1,066.00	$ 68.00	$ 232.50	$ 6,493.00	19
27	$ 1,110.00	$ 8,798.00	$ 480.00	$ 225.00	$ 285.00	$ 10,898.00	35
28	$ 927.00	$ 777.00	$ 1,203.00	$ 284.00	$ 62.00	$ 3,253.00	11
29	$ 1,262.00	$ 1,005.00	$ 1,072.00	$ -	$ 125.00	$ 3,464.00	13
30	$ 770.10	$ -	$ 749.00	$ -	$ 463.90	$ 1,983.00	8
31	$ 1,608.50	$ 497.00	$ 4,445.00	$ -	$ 168.50	$ 6,719.00	23
			$ 36,506.51				
	$ 24,630.87	$ 28,832.49	$ 34,316.12	$ 8,615.00	$ 7,215.13	$ 103,609.61	350

Average per Day	$ 3,412.90			Real Income		$ 87,779.48	

As you can see, I can establish indicators with these values. The data gathering would allow me to evaluate hoy my clients are paying. Which days were more profitable, days of the week where we had high or low patient traffic.

Ok, you are able to establish some financial indicators with your daily sales. But what about the patient information? What kind of data can you gather that will help you to get to know your clients and allow you to make better decisions or create a strategy?

Well, from the daily data (Figure A – Client Data in Daily Sales) I create a consolidated file that puts ALL the days into one excel sheet. And with that, I create a table that allows me to analyze the information. Where I can filter, organize and analyze the data so I can review which clients came during the month, what they purchased (the service provided) and

No.	Costumer	Pet	Dr.	Assistant	Servike	Innvoice	ment M	TEL	Email	New or Retan
5/6/2013 ABIGAIL DE ORELLANA					Recargo	2893	EF			
5/6/2013 ABIGAIL DE ORELLANA	MIETTE	LUIS	GUST	Tratamiento	2933	EF			
5/7/2013 ABIGAIL DE ORELLANA	MIETTE	LUIS	GUYT	Tratamiento	2933	EF			
5/27/2013 ABNER XOT				Recargo	3160	TC	abnerk3.@hotmail.com		
5/27/2013 ABNER XOT	PELUSA	MILDRE	JOSUE	Tratamiento	3160	TC	abnerk3.@hotmail.com	Nuevo
5/1/2013 Adolfo Aleman	DRACO	MOR	ORI	TRATAMIENTO	2856	EF		Reconsulta
5/8/2013 ALBA DE ORDONEZ				Rayos X	2946	TC		
5/8/2013 ALBA DE ORDONEZ	PERRO	MOR	JOSUE	Tratamiento	2946	TC	albabrvas@hotmail.com	Nuevo
5/1/2013 ALEISA QUIROA				Recargo	2851	EF	54178613 a.quiroa10@gmail.com	Nuevo
5/1/2013 ALEISA QUIROA	CHATI	FER	JOSUE	Tratamiento	2851	EF	a.quiroa10@gmail.com	Nuevo
5/18/2013 ALEJANDRA GALVEZ	ANGIE			Bath	3035	EF	NO TIENEN	Reconsulta
5/20/2013 ALEJANDRA NOWELL	LUCAS	MOR	JOSUE	MULTIPLE+RABIA	3088	TC	3530-9123	Reconsulta
5/9/2013 ALEJANDRO MELGAR				Bath	2944	CH	sonia142@hotmail.com	Nuevo
5/9/2013 ALEJANDRO MELGAR				hospedaje	2944	CH	24784083 sonia142@hotmail.com	Reconsulta
5/9/2013 ALEJANDRO MELGAR	BRUNO	FER		Tratamiento	2944	CH	sonia142@hotmail.com	Nuevo
5/17/2013 ALEJANDRO VILLEGAS	KIMBA	MIL	***	Bath	3048	TC		
5/17/2013 ALEJANDRO VILLEGAS				Consulta	3048	TC		Reconsulta
5/17/2013 ALEJANDRO VILLEGAS				Desparacitacion	3048	TC		
5/28/2013 ALICE PERRY DE FARK	HERSEY	MOR	FER	Outlay Puntos		0		
5/8/2013 ALMA GONZALEZ	SCRAPY	MOR	JOSUE	1º RABIA	2947	TC		
5/8/2013 ALMA GONZALEZ	NEGRITO			Tratamiento	2947	TC		
5/25/2013 AMANDA JUDITH LOPEZ	ARTURO			Bath	3145	TC		Reconsulta
5/11/2013 AMILCAR BARRIOS	COQUI			Bath	2980	EF		
5/24/2013 AMILCAR BARRIOS	COQUI	MOR	JOSUE	Tratamiento	3134	TC		Reconsulta
5/31/2013 AMILCAR BARRIOS				Bath	3209	EF		Reconsulta
5/31/2013 AMILCAR BARRIOS	COQUI	MOR	ORI	Consulta	3209	EF		
5/1/2013 AMILCAR CAJAS	MUÑECA	MOR	FER:IRENE	AGL	2977	TC		
5/1/2013 AMILCAR CAJAS				Cirugia	2977	TC		

any contact information if I need to reach them.

In this case, the information is ordered by clients' name, allowing me to view who returned during the month, why, and I can see in the Dr. column, who provided the service. (Allowing me to evaluate my employee performance)

I can organize the information in any way I want, by date, service provided, client, payment method or any variable that will help me decide how to create promotions, evaluate my employee performance, list the best-selling services, etc.

A very important indicator is in column "O" where it says "New or Return" – That indicator allows me to evaluate how many new customers came back, and how many are new. That is a KEY PERFORMANCE INDICATOR that will let me evaluate if my customers are returning and if I am attracting new business.

This type of information can be gathered within a month, or you can extend the period. For example, six months:

Date	Client		Pet Name	Dr.	Assistan	Service	TEL	Email	New or Retu
10-Mar	ABEL ESTUARDO LIMA		REMI	LUIS	JOSUE	TX	41282743	no tiene	Reconsulta
27-Jan	ADELA CASTILLO		KISSY			BCU	49476015	azucenagarcia306@gmail.com	Reconsulta
7-Mar	ADELA CASTILLO		TITO	****	****	BAÑO/CORTE	55150587	azucenagarcia306@gmail.com	Reconsulta
14-Apr	AEMS (MI SILENCIO) /KARLA CHACON		PERRO/OJO			ABONO/IBM	59668721	no tiene	Reconsulta
9-Jun	AEMS LUCERO MORALES		VIEJO PASTOR INGLES	MOR	GUSTAVO	ABONO	42307553		Reconsult
24-May	AFRICA ESTEBANEZ		MASTER			BCU	24432204	franciscoupun@hotmail.com	Reconsulta
1-Mar	AFRICA ESTEBAÑEZ		MASTER	****	****	BCU	2442204	franciscoupunhotmfail.com	Reconsulta
27-Jan	AIDE CHENG HEALY					CONS	40709606	no tiene	Reconsulta
15-Jul	ALEMA IRENE MEJIA		FIRULAY			BAÑO	57850860		Reconsulta
28-Apr	ALBA MIRIAM PAZ		TOFFY	MOR	JOSUE	RABIA	55589205	licdamiriampaz@yahoo.es	Reconsulta
28-Apr	ALBA MIRIAM PAZ					BAÑO	55589205	licdamiriampaz@yahoo.es	Reconsulta
25-Jan	ALBEL ESTUARDO LIMA					RECARGO	41282743	no tiene	Reconsulta
26-Apr	ALBERTO COY LOPEZ		PRINCESA	FER	JOSUE	CONS	51920319	NO TIENE	Reconsulta
17-Feb	ALBERTO REYES/ANDREA REYES					RECARGO	58024575	no tiene	Reconsulta
1-May	ALDA DE LEON					DES		delegnaldo8@gmail.com	Reconsulta
21-Jun	ALDO DE LEON		CANELO	MOR	JOSUE	MULTIPLE	27921845	delegnaldo8@gmail.com	Reconsult
5-Jul	ALDO DE LEON		CANELO	MOR	JOSUE	RABIA	22512695	delegnaldo8@gmail.com	Reconsulta
20-May	ALDO DE LEON		GUANTES	LUIS	JOSUE	Consulta	52054664	no tiene	Reconsulta
13-Mar	ALEJANDRA CASTAÑEDA		COCO	LOURDES	****	1/2CONSULTA	43496903	alejandrac_1402@hotmail.com	RE
1-Apr	ALEJANDRA CASTAÑEDA		OREO	LUIS	JOSUE	CONSULTA	30322475	alejandrac_1402@hotmail.com	Reconsulta
1-Apr	ALEJANDRA CASTAÑEDA					HOSPITAL	30322475	alejandrac_1402@hotmail.com	Reconsulta
21-May	ALEJANDRA CASTAÑEDA		OREO	MOR	ORLANDO	Consulta	30332475	alejandrac_1402@hotmail.com	Reconsulta
18-Jan	ALEJANDRA GALVEZ		ANGIE	MORALES	ORLANDO	1/2 CONSULTA	20311003	alegalvezr@gmail.com	Reconsulta
15-Mar	ALEJANDRA GALVEZ		ANGIE	****	****	Baño, corte, uñas	56302018	alegalvezr@gmail.com	Reconsulta

Consolidado Enero a Julio   Sheet1   (+)

This following example, gathers the 6 month data from sales. And with it I can analyze the customers that returned within that period. That will allow me to filter the ones that did not return and create a campaign with an offer to get them to return.

That is just ONE of the actions that can originate from this data. I can plan campaigns, reward loyal customers. Monitor my employee performance and more importantly – the company's performance.

Some indicators I used were:

- Number of New clients / Number of Returning Clients

- Clients per service (For example, how many vaccines we provided within that period)

- Employee performance (Clients served by employee)

- NON returning clients within 6 months. (Printed out a list, analyzed the service provided and figured out if I could offer them something to return)

Performance indicators for the company:

PATIENTS PER MONTH						
YEAR	January	February	March	April	May	June
2014	292	311	354	355	367	322
2013	375	344	299	337	352	303
2012	283	293	318	300	315	315

SALES						
2014	$ 105,483.64	$ 97,190.85	$ 119,647.33	$ 106,902.36	$ 115,573.04	$ 113,915.38
2013	$ 123,548.08	$ 108,425.19	$ 108,228.85	$ 111,690.35	$ 118,211.72	$ 104,907.25
2012	$ 88,299.57	$ 74,431.05	$ 83,795.11	$ 84,868.69	$ 91,405.95	$ 92,725.45

AVERAGE CONSUMPTION - INCOME PER MONTH PER CUSTOMER						
2014	$ 361.25	$ 312.51	$ 337.99	$ 301.13	$ 314.91	$ 353.77
2013	$ 329.46	$ 315.19	$ 361.97	$ 331.43	$ 335.83	$ 346.23
2012	$ 312.01	$ 254.03	$ 263.51	$ 282.90	$ 290.18	$ 294.37

PATIENTS PER MONTH							
YEAR	July	August	September	October	November	December	TOTAL PATIENTS
2014	318	299	278	273	297	311	3777
2013	308	271	253	331	307	318	3798
2012	350	296	303	309	276	306	3664

SALES							
2014	$ 112,859.00	$ 99,438.00	$ 105,461.30	$ 101,765.00	$ 98,475.00	$ 109,776.00	$ 1,286,486.90
2013	$ 114,124.50	$ 80,171.25	$ 99,423.02	$ 102,649.75	$ 102,305.21	$ 105,329.03	$ 1,279,014.20
2012	$ 99,983.60	$ 94,263.25	$ 92,548.30	$ 104,252.75	$ 82,816.01	$ 84,951.10	$ 1,074,340.83

AVERAGE CONSUMPTION - INCOME PER MONTH PER CUSTOMER							
2014	$ 354.90	$ 332.57	$ 379.36	$ 372.77	$ 331.57	$ 352.98	$ 340.61
2013	$ 370.53	$ 295.83	$ 392.98	$ 310.12	$ 333.24	$ 331.22	$ 336.76
2012	$ 285.67	$ 318.46	$ 305.44	$ 337.39	$ 300.06	$ 277.62	$ 293.22

As a small company, I have to evaluate what I have been able to achieve and how that compares to previous periods. As we´ve seen, with excel, I can gather data that allows me to control, how many clients per day, how much they purchase on average and with that I can create a simple report that will define if I am doing better or worse. Yearly Analysis:

With this information I can compare my results from previous years and establish I am being able to grow and become more profitable. As you can see, my average consumption varies a lot, but I have been able to increase it. BUT as you can see the number of patients reduced from 2013 to 2014. That kind of information allows me to plan. See how it can be VERY important?

CHAPTER 5
SMALL BUSINESS FINANCE

Budget and Results

A business that monitors where the money is assigned to go is better prepared to make decisions. A budget allows you to control and plan effectively in regards to your assets and resources. Additionally it lists in detail the financial responsibilities of your company.

Small companies that do not place importance in budgeting, may increase the risk of spending more than you generate. Or not investing enough for your company to grow.

A small business needs the ability to adapt to changes generated by the market, the economy, and the local factors that might influence the results you may obtain at any period of time. Because of that, uncertainty is part of the game, and one of the key aspects you need to be prepared for uncertainty is a proper budget for operating your business.

A budget can assist you in preparing for the future, learning from the past and give you the ability to control your company. It will present management with important information needed for the right decisions at the right time.

The brief information we are going to review will assist and guide you to know the basic areas within your finances; areas such as forecasting, preparing a cash flow, a profit and loss statement and balance sheet budgets.

Benefits you can obtain by preparing a budget for your company:

- **Performance Monitoring:** with a budget you can compare your expected results (forecast) with the actual results in a period. This will allow you to evaluate the areas that might need improvement and help you make decisions for the future.

- *Effective Financial Management:* Without a budget you run the risk of spending additional money that was not necessary, or spending less that planned and affecting your results.

- *Obtaining a business loan or investors:* If you manage a strict and accurate budget, you possess a tool that can demonstrate to a financial institution or potential investment that you have managed your expenses, calculated your revenues and you can afford a loan payment if necessary.

- *Your own Benchmark:* A supervised and accurate budget can help you set and reach financial goals for your company.

Factors to consider in budgeting applied to your company:

- Get the adequate people involved. Share or clarify relevant information with employees that work and lead the different areas of your company. (Purchasing, Marketing, distribution, operations.)

- Assign budget responsibility only if the person has the authority to influence and manage the outcome.

- Using the previous years of operation as a guide is a viable option for creating a realistic budget.

- Take time to analyze all your departments, what expense they represent in your budget and try to create a general budget that can set the benchmark for all other budgets.

- To acquire the actual data you can create a spreadsheet template that contains all the relevant information on expenses, purchases and all the budget information. Once the spreadsheet is created you can fill the data or give them to the individuals in charge who can provide you with accurate and real information.

PREPARING A BASIC BUDGET:

A business budget can vary in the type of information they can provide a company. It is necessary to define and ensure that the one you prepare is suited to your business objectives.

There are three main types:

- *Profit and Loss Statement:* This budget type requires you to calculate your company sales and expenses for a determined period. With this type of budget you are able to evaluate the results of your operation and establish targets for income and profits you would like to earn.

- *Cash Flow Budget:* This type of budget is a plan you can outline where you detail your company's expected income and outflow of cash for a period of time. This is based on estimating all types of resources coming into your company and providing capital, like sales, loans, and other cash income. At the same time you can detail all your expected expenses, like payroll, commissions, bonuses, purchase inventory and any other operating expenses.

- *Projected Balance Sheet:* This information will outline all of your company's assets and list projected liabilities. It is created with the objective of detailing where the money originates from (loans, cash reserves, fixed assets, accumulated profits, etc.) and where it is planned to be spent. (Fixed assets, stocks, investments, debts, reserves, acquisitions, etc.)

  The balance sheet is to specify the current situation and provide a picture of the company's performance in a specific period or point in time.

Considerations for preparing a budget:

- You require a guide to assist you in cost and sales; if historical figures are available, they can serve as a great element to anticipate every factor you consider important in the operation, and you can use them to be realistic with your budget. Remember that historical data are just a base, they cannot represent what will happen, as market conditions and circumstances can and have changed.

- Try to involved key personnel or people who have experience and knowledge in the business or are financially savvy. Staff members and experienced individuals can provide useful input when trying to establish realistic numbers. And also, they can provide you with the necessary facts to determine if your goals are attainable.

- o When key employees within your company are involved, they can become motivated in setting and helping to achieve the goals established.

- Prepare or always consider variables. In any business environment and operation, there can and most likely will be, unforeseen expenses. That is something you might have to deal with at some point during your operation. Because of this, it is a good idea to assign some funds to an account so you can be prepared if any unexpected expenses arise.

When preparing a Budget be sure to include:

- Accounts payable, what type of suppliers provide you credit? When will they have to be paid?

- Do you offer credit to special costumers? When do they pay?

- Do you pay anything in advance? E.g. Insurance premiums?

- Any financial or fiscal responsibilities, like paying loans and taxes. Also any dividends you are planning to pay.

One of the main objectives of budgets, is to show you projected profits for a period of time. At the same time it is an evaluation of your level of control of all the areas within the company. If the budgets are very similar to the results, then, your overall control of information and results will demonstrate you know and control pretty much every area of operation.

If the budget and results vary dramatically, you have to analyze the exact area where the changes and variations occurred, if this is not caused by something completely unforeseen and out of your control, then you have to determine where you miscalculated or lacked the information needed to make an adequate budget.

BUDGET EXAMPLES

Cash Flow Budget - Results

This is a budget example for a quarter. As you can see, we factor all the key variables to establish what was spent in operation and what income

YOUR COMPANY					
Cash Flow Budget QTR 1					
	January		February		March
Opening Balance	$	9,000.00	$	33,677.25	$	51,119.00
Cash Inflows					
Sales receipts	$	67,475.00	$	88,575.00	$	80,025.00
Business Loan	$	15,000.00	$	-	$	-
Intrest Payment	$	250.00	$	250.00	$	250.00
Other income	$	15,250.00	$	250.00	$	250.00
Total Cash Inflows	$	**91,725.00**	$	**122,502.25**	$	**131,394.00**
- Cash Outflows					
Purchases of inventory	$	13,052.50	$	17,816.25	$	15,629.75
Salaries & Wages	$	32,750.00	$	41,250.00	$	41,250.00
Marketing	$	2,450.00	$	2,450.00	$	3,950.00
Taxes	$	8,446.50	$	10,940.50	$	10,171.00
Business Loan Payment	$	-	$	1,200.00	$	1,200.00
Other expenses	$	750.00	$	20,750.00	$	1,550.00
Savings Account	$	3,373.75	$	4,428.75	$	4,001.25
Total Cash Outflows	$	**67,047.75**	$	**105,060.50**	$	**83,977.00**
Closing Balance	$	**33,677.25**	$	**51,119.00**	$	**98,536.00**

was perceived.

When you create a budget, these totals can guide you to where you are spending more than you should and where the income is coming from. But in this example we only view the totals, or end results. To create an accurate budget, you have to go into detail. So you can evaluate your expenses on a monthly bases and see your results.

It is critical to create a budget, start with one that SIMULATES what you expect to happen. And as the results come in, you have to COMPARE the simulation with the actual figures at the end of the month. A detailed Cash Flow Budget has to consider all the variables for income and outcome of cash. You have to structure the information in an ordered manner so it is easy to fill out, supervise and analyze.

Cash Flow Budget - Details

In this example you can see the same budget, but in detail for every department, product, and variable.

	YOUR COMPANY							
	Cash Flow Budget QTR 1							
	January			February			March	
Opening Balance	$	9,000.00	$		33,677.25	$		51,119.00
Cash Inflows								
	Quantity	$ Value		Quantity	$ Value		Quantity	$ Value
Product A	25	$ 5,875.00		30	$ 7,050.00		15	$ 3,525.00
Product B	50	$ 11,750.00		60	$ 14,100.00		55	$ 12,925.00
Product C	50	$ 21,750.00		75	$ 32,625.00		70	$ 30,450.00
Client Type A Service	20	$ 14,700.00		20	$ 14,700.00		20	$ 14,700.00
Client Type B Service	40	$ 13,400.00		60	$ 20,100.00		55	$ 18,425.00
Sales receipts	$	67,475.00	$		88,575.00	$		80,025.00
Business Loan	$	15,000.00	$		-	$		-
Intrest Payment	$	250.00	$		250.00	$		250.00
Other income	$	15,250.00	$		250.00	$		250.00
Total Cash Inflows	$	91,725.00	$		122,502.25	$		131,394.00
- Cash Outflows								
	Quantity	Cost		Quantity	Cost		Quantity	Cost
Product A	25	$ 1,762.50		30	$ 2,115.00		15	$ 1,057.50
Product B	50	$ 4,112.50		60	$ 4,935.00		55	$ 4,523.75
Product C	50	$ 7,177.50		75	$ 10,766.25		70	$ 10,048.50
Purchases of inventory	$	13,052.50	$		17,816.25	$		15,629.75
	Base Salary	Other (Commissions, Expenses, Bonus, etc.)		Base Salary	Other (Commissions, Expenses, Bonus, etc.)		Base Salary	Other (Commissions, Expenses, Bonus, etc.)
John Smith	$ 7,500.00	$ -		$ 7,500.00	$ -		$ 7,500.00	$ -
Jeff Fontana	$ 4,750.00			$ 4,750.00			$ 4,750.00	
Nicole Hill	$ 3,500.00	$ 1,000.00		$ 3,500.00	$ 1,000.00		$ 3,500.00	$ 1,000.00
Ana Jacobs	$ 3,500.00	$ 1,000.00		$ 3,500.00	$ 1,000.00		$ 3,500.00	$ 1,000.00
Josh Andersen	$ 3,500.00	$ 1,000.00		$ 3,500.00	$ 1,000.00		$ 3,500.00	$ 1,000.00
Jill Mathers	$ 4,000.00	$ 500.00		$ 4,000.00	$ 500.00		$ 4,000.00	$ 500.00
Stacy Williams	$ -	$ -		$ 4,000.00	$ 500.00		$ 4,000.00	$ 500.00
Andrew Johnson	$ -	$ -		$ 4,000.00	$ -		$ 4,000.00	$ -
Accounting	$ 2,500.00	$ -		$ 2,500.00	$ -		$ 2,500.00	$ -
Salaries & Wages	$	32,750.00	$		41,250.00	$		41,250.00
Rent / Mortgage	$	3,250.00	$		3,250.00	$		3,250.00
Telecomunications	$	475.00	$		475.00	$		475.00
Electric	$	750.00	$		750.00	$		750.00
Water and Gas	$	250.00	$		250.00	$		250.00
Maintenance	$	600.00	$		600.00	$		600.00
Cleaning Services	$	900.00	$		900.00	$		900.00
Utilities	$	6,225.00	$		6,225.00	$		6,225.00

Cash Flow Budget – Details (Cont.)

	January		February		March
YOUR COMPANY					
Cash Flow Budget QTR 1					
Utilities	$	6,225.00	$	6,225.00	$ 6,225.00
Magazine Ad	$	900.00	$	900.00	$ 900.00
Facebook Marketing	$	150.00	$	150.00	$ 150.00
Google Marketing	$	150.00	$	150.00	$ 150.00
Radio Ad	$	1,000.00	$	1,000.00	$ 1,000.00
Event	$	-	$	-	$ 1,500.00
Other Marketing	$	250.00	$	250.00	$ 250.00
Marketing	$	2,450.00	$	2,450.00	$ 3,950.00
Sales Taxes	$	6,072.75	$	7,971.75	$ 7,202.25
Property Taxes	$	81.25	$	81.25	$ 81.25
Employees	$	2,292.50	$	2,887.50	$ 2,887.50
Taxes	$	8,446.50	$	10,940.50	$ 10,171.00
Business Loan Payment	$	-	$	1,200.00	$ 1,200.00
Deliver Van Purchase	$	-	$	20,000.00	$ -
Delivery Van Maintenance	$	-	$	-	$ 500.00
Insurance	$	750.00	$	750.00	$ 1,050.00
Other expenses	$	750.00	$	20,750.00	$ 1,550.00
Savings Account	$	3,373.75	$	4,428.75	$ 4,001.25
Total Cash Outflows	$	**67,047.75**	$	**105,060.50**	$ **83,977.00**
Closing Balance	$	**33,677.25**	$	**51,119.00**	$ **98,536.00**

It is the same budget as you saw in the results, just with every detail and expense that will influence your result.

If you do a projection budget, it will allow you to evaluate what will come in and what it will cost. You could do it for a semester, and on a quarterly basis, evaluate the results. Compare the budget with the actual data generated by your business.

Budgeting Assistance Tips:

If you have a good relationship with your bank, and if you have an account manager, you can ask them if they have any software or training they can assist you with. Banks have special people to review and evaluate budgets, and they can give you tools or tips on how to create yours accurately.

A lot of people have the necessary skills to create a good budget, but when it comes to preparing balance sheets, profit and loss statements or in depth analysis, they lack the knowledge required to generate or evaluate the data.

For this, there are a lot of accounting software that can be helpful for your company but if will not be a useful tool if you do not have the skill to use it.

Try reaching to your local small business organization, or your accounting company, they can provide you with the training needed for you to learn how to use a software properly or how to create the budgets you require, but more importantly, how to create balance sheets that are linked to your profit- loss statements and cash flow budget. And more importantly how to analyze and use the data to make the right decisions for your company.

Using a Consolidated budget to manage cash flow and prepare for the future budgeting periods

- Once you have established a consolidated budget you have to establish the frequency of revision it will require to help you make decisions or apply changes.

- A once a month review of the projected budget versus the actual expenses can help you a system to pin point areas where you present variances.

- Budget management practices will allow you to evaluate your performance, detect potential problems and reduce the reaction time required to solve unforeseen problems.

- Create a yearly budget if possible, or quarterly budget. And as soon as the month ends you need to receive the reports needed to compare to your budget.

- Establish key performance indicators to evaluate your results in an efficient manner how your operation is doing.

SALES FORCASTING

This is a process your company has to use to try and predict the future sales of your products and services. The main idea is to try and create projections of what you will sell and have a historical base to support it. Your past sales history can serve as a base for your forecast, but trying to replicate results based on your sales history is very inefficient. The market conditions and YOUR company situation a year ago or two, were very different from what they will be in your next period.

This is why accurate sales forecasts use historical data for a starting point, but evaluate all the variables and considerations needed to establish or simulate what will happen. (Will new potential clients open in your area? Do you plan to hire more sales reps? Are you going to start providing products or services in other regions? What if a major client leaves your region and you no longer count on that costumer?)

A sales forecast has to consider market analysis, trends, sales person's estimates or historical data and everything you will deem important to set achievable goals and generate the sales revenue you need to grow.

Variations that can arise when planning and compared with your past sales are:

- Market changes and industry trends

- New competitors

- Marketing strategies

- Product or service pricing variation

- Launch of new products or services

- New personnel

- New territory

- Key client acquisition

- Important client loss

A sales forecast will help you evaluate the resources you currently have at your disposal, and help you determine how they will be used or how they will vary.

- If you use direct sales and visit potential customers:

  - What sales method will you use? Will you vary the strategy in any way?

  - How many costumers do you currently have? What type of costumers are they? Are they classified?

  - How many current customers will you visit, and what sales do you expect from current clients? What repeat business do you expect? Do you already have confirmed orders?

  - How many potential customers will you contact and what rate of success do you expect form your visits?

- Do you have any marketing campaigns planned? How many leads or inquiries will that generate? What percentage of those do you expect to turn into sales?

Separate Forecasting:

- Depending on how many teams and areas you need to cover, and how many goals you have to set, you may want to build of different forecasts for different regions, services, products or even employees.

- This will assist you in establishing:

  - Individual performance by territory, employee, etc.

  - Evaluate product or services profitability.

  - Guidelines to identify problem areas.

COSTS FORCASTING

This is a process your company has to use after trying to try and predict the future sales of your products and services. The main idea is to try and create projections that will help you establish a baseline of what that will cost.

You can establish a cost forecast in a fixed or variable amount. Related to your operation and / or desired results.

A fixed cost forecast or budget will be structured independently from your level of sales, you will take in account every programmable and continuous expense you can list. Assign the values and establish a monthly budget you can supervise and measure.

A variable cost budget will be linked to the number of sales or inventory turnover. It can include distribution costs for example, that will be part of the turnover. These variables can assist you in establishing a cost per sale. The ideal situation is to create a combination of both types of budgets. Developing this type of budget that can include fixed and variable expenses.

A Cost budget will allow you to analyze your costs and expenses and determine how they relate to sales and income. You may have a great idea and control on your current expenses, and may even feel this is not something that might help you in much, but a good budget can allow you to track your performance and where all the money is going. This will prepare you to identify unexpected variables that might force you to change your pricing, or simply stated, determine if your profits are being spent on areas that could be improved, or the costs reduced.

Your cost forecasting should include:

- Fixed expenses to operate

  - Utilities

  - Rent

  - Payroll

  - Insurance – etc.

- Variable costs

  - Inventory Purchases

  - Sales commissions

  - Taxes - etc.

Analyzing your budgets

After you are able to establish your sales and costs forecasting, your company will have the opportunity to prevent potential risks before they happen. It will allow you to compare your planned and variable expenses with the potential income you expect to receive.

This strategy can enable your company to set goals, supervise performance and plan your income position month by month.

Creating and analyzing your budget will define the following objectives:

- Define your limits on spending

  - Knowing your income and outcome timeline will obligate you to invest or spend where there is potential risk.

- Evaluate your cash position

  - If the position is extremely variable you will want to establish shorter time periods in your cash flow to determine where the problem is located or what measures you need to take to be prepared.

- Establish adequate margins for your products and/or services

  - If your expenses are close to your income limits you may need to take action that could lead to increasing prices, evaluate cost reduction strategies.

- Determine if your company is not being profitable and how you can reach a breakeven level of turnover.

  - If capital is growing faster than your sales, you need to establish control points to reduce the risk of over spending.

- Compare your projections to the results of previous years.

  - This is key to identifying the different areas within your business that have improved or deteriorated.

  - Products or services that are underperforming, clients that have reduced their spending with your company, etc.

- SALES VERSUS EXPENSES:

  - When performing an evaluation of your expenses versus your potential income, you have to consider that the expenses can vary according to your sales results, but at the same time, your income will be influenced directly by several factors that might change your sales results. With that in mind, you may want to prepare 3 types of budgets:

- Most likely scenario: imagine your sales will be the same or very close to your previous years.

- Pessimistic scenario: certain aspects of your business will suffer from something you already know or suspect. A big client leaving, a change in your local market, a new competitor, etc.

- Optimistic: all your goals and growth strategies are achieved and you generate additional income compared to previous years without spending more or increasing your costs significantly.

CHAPTER 6

Growth in Sales versus Growth in Profits:

Many companies are content with a steady growth in sales every year, they are like clockwork and can be averaged out to, let's say, an average of 10% increase every year.

That may be fantastic results if achieved without putting your profit margins at risk.

For example:

	2012		2013		2014
COMPANY NAME					
Yearly Comparrisson					
Opening Balance	$	9,000.00	$	81,121.25	$	46,285.50
Cash Inflows						
Sales receipts	$	648,600.00	$	736,780.00	$	810,458.00
Business Loan	$	15,000.00	$	-	$	-
Intrest Payment from Savings	$	1,621.50	$	1,841.95	$	2,026.15
Other income	$	16,621.50	$	1,841.95	$	2,026.15
Total Cash Inflows	$	**674,221.50**	$	**819,743.20**	$	**858,769.65**
- Cash Outflows						
Purchases of inventory	$	145,230.00	$	168,283.50	$	211,556.40
Salaries & Wages	$	333,000.00	$	510,750.00	$	545,887.50
Utilities	$	6,225.00	$	6,372.50	$	6,534.75
Marketing	$	2,700.00	$	3,240.00	$	3,888.00
Taxes	$	81,765.25	$	102,143.95	$	111,234.60
Business Loan Payment	$	-	$	1,200.00	$	1,200.00
Other expenses	$	750.00	$	25,750.00	$	9,750.00
Savings Account	$	32,430.00	$	36,839.00	$	40,522.90
Total Cash Outflows	$	**602,100.25**	$	**854,578.95**	$	**930,574.15**
Closing Balance	$	**81,121.25**	$	**46,285.50**	$	**(25,519.00)**

A budget analysis will help your company establish where the impact is located in your operation, with that, you will be able to determine the risk to your company and the effects of any changes to significant variances in operational costs and sales performance.

If we see the budget, every year the **Sales Receipts** line clearly shows that every year the sales increased by a 10% margin. Having a direct results with the Cash Inflows line.

Additionally you can see how the sales receipts will influence the purchase of inventory. The more you sell, the more you have to buy. And that is pretty much in line with the results obtained.

But why is the closing balance reducing? Why if we increased sales, is our balance being reduced at the end of the year? As you can see, from 81k we went down to 46k and even worse, in the third year, we are in negative.

If we analyze in detail we can evaluate where our problem is located:

Let's review the Inflows:

	COMPANY NAME							
	Yearly Comparrisson							
	2012			2013			2014	
Opening Balance	$	9,000.00	$		81,121.25	$		46,285.50
Cash Inflows								
	Quantity	$ Value		Quantity	$ Value		Quantity	$ Value
Product A	25	$ 70,500.00		27.5	$ 77,550.00		30.25	$ 85,305.00
Product B	55	$ 155,100.00		60.5	$ 170,610.00		66.55	$ 187,671.00
Product C	75	$ 211,500.00		82.5	$ 232,650.00		90.75	$ 255,915.00
Client Type A Service	35	$ 98,700.00		38.5	$ 108,570.00		42.35	$ 119,427.00
Client Type B Service	40	$ 112,800.00		44	$ 147,400.00		48.4	$ 162,140.00
Sales receipts	$	648,600.00	$		736,780.00	$		810,458.00
Business Loan	$	15,000.00	$		-	$		-
Intrest Payment from Savings	$	1,621.50	$		1,841.95	$		2,026.15
Other income	$	16,621.50	$		1,841.95	$		2,026.15
Total Cash Inflows	**$**	**674,221.50**	**$**		**819,743.20**	**$**		**858,769.65**

As you can see in this part of the budget, the sales increased by 10% each year, and that had a direct result on the resources available for your company.

If we consider the results, we can ask ourselves:

- My company is growing, as a result, I have additional resources to invest in my growth.

- What was the key for my growth? What product under performed?

- How can I continue to grow?

- Does my continuing sales growth mean I am more profitable?

If we analyze only the income, the company would seem to be very successful. Steady growth, year after year. And with that additional income, YOU AS THE OWNER start to make decisions. But, are they the correct ones?

It does not matter how much our income has increased from year to year. If we don't compare and ANALYZE it against our expenses. That can lead us to a very dangerous road.

	COMPANY NAME							
	Yearly Comparrisson							
	2012			2013			2014	
Opening Balance	$	9,000.00	$		81,121.25	$		46,285.50
Total Cash Inflows	$	674,221.50	$		819,743.20	$		858,769.65
- Cash Outflows								
	Quantity	Cost		Quantity	Cost		Quantity	Cost
Product A	25	$ 21,150.00		27.5	$ 27,142.50		30.25	$ 34,122.00
Product B	55	$ 54,285.00		60.5	$ 59,713.50		66.55	$ 75,068.40
Product C	75	$ 69,795.00		82.5	$ 81,427.50		90.75	$ 102,366.00
Purchases of inventory	$	145,230.00	$		168,283.50	$		211,556.40
	Base Salary	Other (Commissions, Expenses, Bonus, etc.)		Base Salary	Other (Commissions, Expenses, Bonus, etc.)		Base Salary	Other (Commissions,
John Smith	$90,000.00	$ -		$94,500.00	$ -		$99,225.00	$ -
Jeff Fontana	$57,000.00			$59,850.00			$62,842.50	
Nicole Hill	$42,000.00	$ 12,000.00		$44,100.00	$ 12,000.00		$46,305.00	$ 12,000.00
Ana Jacobs	$ -	$ -		$42,000.00	$ 12,000.00		$44,100.00	$ 12,000.00
Josh Andersen	$ -	$ -		$42,000.00	$ 12,000.00		$44,100.00	$ 12,000.00
Jill Mathers	$48,000.00	$ 6,000.00		$50,400.00	$ 6,000.00		$52,920.00	$ 6,000.00
Stacy Williams	$ -	$ -		$48,000.00	$ 6,000.00		$50,400.00	$ 6,000.00
Andrew Johnson	$48,000.00	$ -		$50,400.00	$ -		$52,920.00	$ 12,000.00
Accounting	$30,000.00	$ -		$31,500.00	$ -		$33,075.00	$ -
Salaries & Wages	$	333,000.00	$		510,750.00	$		545,887.50

Let´s see the rest of the budget:

If we take the Inflows and start analyzing our expenses, we can quickly identify that from 2012 to 2013 we increased the salaries for every employee. And that makes sense, we were successful and profitable, everybody deserves a chance to get more money.

Another difference we can identify is that we hired 3 new employees. (Ana, Josh and Stacy) And if we have a plan for them, well it would make sense to hire more people if we want to grow. And as we can see at the end of the year we grew another 10%. But how about our Salary and Wage expense? Well that increased a whopping 53%!!!

Does that make sense? Why the big increase? And more importantly, why did that increase not have a better effect in my sales?

As you can see, once we have more resources available, we can easily think, hey, I will hire more people to grow more!!! And if we compare our sales receipts from 2012 to 2014, well we increased from 674k to 858k, and that is impressive!!!

But why not more? If I have more people, I would be able to sell more, have more clients, do more and increase my results by MORE than 10%, right?

Rent / Mortgage	$ 3,250.00	$ 3,250.00	$ 3,250.00
Telecomunications	$ 475.00	$ 522.50	$ 574.75
Electric	$ 750.00	$ 825.00	$ 907.50
Water and Gas	$ 250.00	$ 275.00	$ 302.50
Maintenance	$ 600.00	$ 600.00	$ 600.00
Cleaning Services	$ 900.00	$ 900.00	$ 900.00
Utilities	$ 6,225.00	$ 6,372.50	$ 6,534.75
Magazine Ad	$ 900.00	$ 1,080.00	$ 1,296.00
Facebook Marketing	$ 150.00	$ 180.00	$ 216.00
Google Marketing	$ 150.00	$ 180.00	$ 216.00
Radio Ad	$ 1,000.00	$ 1,200.00	$ 1,440.00
Event	$ 250.00	$ 300.00	$ 360.00
Other Marketing	$ 250.00	$ 300.00	$ 360.00
Marketing	$ 2,700.00	$ 3,240.00	$ 3,888.00
Sales Taxes	$ 58,374.00	$ 66,310.20	$ 72,941.22
Property Taxes	$ 81.25	$ 81.25	$ 81.25
Employees	$ 23,310.00	$ 35,752.50	$ 38,212.13
Taxes	$ 81,765.25	$ 102,143.95	$ 111,234.60
Business Loan Payment	$ -	$ 1,200.00	$ 1,200.00
Deliver Van Purchase	$ -	$ 20,000.00	$ -
Delivery Van Maintenance	$ -	$ 5,000.00	$ 9,000.00
Insurance	$ 750.00	$ 750.00	$ 750.00
Other expenses	$ 750.00	$ 25,750.00	$ 9,750.00
Savings Account	$ 32,430.00	$ 36,839.00	$ 40,522.90
Total Cash Outflows	$ 602,100.25	$ 854,578.95	$ 930,574.15
Closing Balance	$ 81,121.25	$ 46,285.50	$ (25,519.00)

If we review our end results, even though our company´s income increased by a lot from 2012 to 2014, our expenses did at an even stronger pace. The bump in salaries and the hiring of new employees. Just 3 more people, but if you add that up, it will take its toll. And you can see in the results, at the end of the year, I am not being able to be profitable. Each year that passes, I have less resources available. And by year 2014, I will start running on red. And ending each year strapped by cash. And even if 2015 my sales increase again, it will not be enough!!!

You can continue to grow, by 10% each year, but if you do not control your expenses, that is when you start to get in trouble.

Don´t believe me? Let´s continue the exercise from 2014 to 2016. And you will see. That at the end of the year my numbers will be even worse.

Continuing from 2014 to 2016

	COMPANY NAME							
	Yearly Comparrisson							
	2014			2015			2016	
Opening Balance	$	46,285.50	$		(25,519.00)	$		(147,332.69)
Cash Inflows								
	Quantity	$ Value		Quantity	$ Value		Quantity	$ Value
Product A	30.25	$ 85,305.00		33.275	$ 93,835.50		36.6025	$ 103,219.05
Product B	66.55	$ 187,671.00		73.205	$ 206,438.10		80.5255	$ 227,081.91
Product C	90.75	$ 255,915.00		99.825	$ 281,506.50		109.8075	$ 309,657.15
Client Type A Service	42.35	$ 119,427.00		46.585	$ 131,369.70		51.2435	$ 144,506.67
Client Type B Service	48.4	$ 162,140.00		53.24	$ 178,354.00		58.564	$ 196,189.40
Sales receipts	$	810,458.00	$		891,503.80	$		980,654.18
Business Loan	$	-	$		-	$		-
Intrest Payment from Savings	$	2,026.15	$		2,228.76	$		2,451.64
Other income	$	2,026.15	$		2,228.76	$		2,451.64
Total Cash Inflows	$	**858,769.65**	$		**868,213.56**	$		**835,773.12**
- Cash Outflows								
	Quantity	Cost		Quantity	Cost		Quantity	Cost
Product A	30.25	$ 34,122.00		33.275	$ 37,534.20		36.6025	$ 41,287.62
Product B	66.55	$ 75,068.40		73.205	$ 82,575.24		80.5255	$ 90,832.76
Product C	90.75	$ 102,366.00		99.825	$ 112,602.60		109.8075	$ 123,862.86
Purchases of inventory	$	211,556.40	$		232,712.04	$		255,983.24
	Base Salary	Other (Commissions,		Base Salary	Other (Commissions,		Base Salary	Other (Commissions,
John Smith	$99,225.00	$ -		$104,186.25	$ -		$109,395.56	$ -
Jeff Fontana	$62,842.50			$ 65,984.63			$ 69,283.86	
Nicole Hill	$46,305.00	$ 12,000.00		$ 48,620.25	$ 12,000.00		$ 51,051.26	$ 12,000.00
Ana Jacobs	$44,100.00	$ 12,000.00		$ 46,305.00	$ 12,000.00		$ 48,620.25	$ 12,000.00
Josh Andersen	$44,100.00	$ 12,000.00		$ 46,305.00	$ 12,000.00		$ 48,620.25	$ 12,000.00
Jill Mathers	$52,920.00	$ 6,000.00		$ 55,566.00	$ 6,000.00		$ 58,344.30	$ 6,000.00
Stacy Williams	$50,400.00	$ 6,000.00		$ 52,920.00	$ 6,000.00		$ 55,566.00	$ 6,000.00
Andrew Johnson	$52,920.00	$ 12,000.00		$ 55,566.00	$ 12,000.00		$ 58,344.30	$ 12,000.00
Accounting	$33,075.00	$ -		$ 34,728.75	$ -		$ 36,465.19	$ -
Salaries & Wages	$	545,887.50	$		570,181.88	$		595,690.97

	2014	2015	2016
Rent / Mortgage	$ 3,250.00	$ 3,250.00	$ 3,250.00
Telecomunications	$ 574.75	$ 632.23	$ 695.45
Electric	$ 907.50	$ 998.25	$ 1,098.08
Water and Gas	$ 302.50	$ 332.75	$ 366.03
Maintenance	$ 600.00	$ 600.00	$ 600.00
Cleaning Services	$ 900.00	$ 900.00	$ 900.00
Utilities	$ 6,534.75	$ 6,713.23	$ 6,909.55
Magazine Ad	$ 1,296.00	$ 1,555.20	$ 1,866.24
Facebook Marketing	$ 216.00	$ 259.20	$ 311.04
Google Marketing	$ 216.00	$ 259.20	$ 311.04
Radio Ad	$ 1,440.00	$ 1,728.00	$ 2,073.60
Event	$ 360.00	$ 432.00	$ 518.40
Other Marketing	$ 360.00	$ 432.00	$ 518.40
Marketing	$ 3,888.00	$ 4,665.60	$ 5,598.72
Sales Taxes	$ 72,941.22	$ 80,235.34	$ 88,258.88
Property Taxes	$ 81.25	$ 81.25	$ 81.25
Employees	$ 38,212.13	$ 39,912.73	$ 41,698.37
Taxes	$ 111,234.60	$ 120,229.32	$ 130,038.49
Business Loan Payment	$ 1,200.00	$ 1,200.00	$ 1,200.00
Deliver Van Purchase	$ -	$ -	$ -
Delivery Van Maintenance	$ 9,000.00	$ 9,000.00	$ 9,000.00
Insurance	$ 750.00	$ 750.00	$ 750.00
Other expenses	$ 9,750.00	$ 9,750.00	$ 9,750.00
Savings Account	$ 40,522.90	$ 44,575.19	$ 49,032.71
Total Cash Outflows	$ 930,574.15	$ 990,027.25	$ 1,054,203.68
Closing Balance	$ (25,519.00)	$ (147,332.69)	$ (365,763.26)

You see? The results are even worse!!! Even though we are increasing, if you take 2012 we had 648k in sales and in 2016 we had 980k. That is more than 300k in difference!

And in 2012 I had 81k in the bank to end the year, and by the end of 2016, I need an extra 365k just to pay the bills? Where do I get the money? What do I do?

If you see part of the budget includes savings, and if I am able to save every year, by 2014 I will not be able to save anything, and that is when a small company can get into trouble!!! BIG TROUBLE!!!

And the major difference? Hiring 3 people and increasing salaries by 5% per year to all employees.

It doesn't sound like a lot, but if you see the big picture, that will bankrupt this company. Easily.

This is why a budget and projection can help you. They can avoid this type of disaster!!!

What key factors could save the company?

Well, if we go back to 2013 when you hired 3 new employees, you need to establish:

- What will my goals be now that I know that I will have 3 new employees? How can they influence my results? What do we need to achieve to continue to grow and be profitable?

- How much time do I give them to show me those results? Am I clear of what I expect them to do? What they need to achieve? Are they clear themselves?

- What happens if instead of a 5% increase we just give out a bonus, depending on the results, I come up with a figure of the closing balance and distribute it proportionally among all the team?

That type of analysis of a budget can SAVE a company! And that is why an employee profile, and goals are so important for a company!!!

Special considerations when evaluating performance and results:

- What happens if one or two of your clients represent a major percentage of your income and there is a major change in their operation and have to leave you as a client? (Relocation, cost reduction, cheaper suppliers, etc.)

- If your volume changes dramatically on one or several products because of your suppliers? (Changes in pricing, delivery dates, production capability, competition, etc.)

- If your results are based on the performance of a specific product or service, how do you maintain it? How to keep the pace?

- If you have several locations, is any of them underperforming specifically? (Location, sales territory, etc.)

- The increase in sales caused to external factors of the season, a special event in your city, a corporate event that required your product or services, what month was the increase and will it be repeated? Can it be repeated?

- Were your targets adequate? Too high or too low?

- Did you close sales earlier than expected? Orders anticipated that benefit your current month but will affect the outcome of the upcoming months?

- Did your costumers fall back on payments? Did you have to pay something upfront?

Actual Expenses:

One of the benefits of evaluating budgets can help you develop the ability to prepare your company for future expenses and potential income in an accurate and organized manner.

As your levels of business increase or decrease you can track your variable costs and make sure your fixed costs do not become too expensive for your company's operation.

It is imperative you follow up on all the variables included in your budgets, this will assist you in establishing simple, yet effective Key Performance Indicators (KPI´s) for your business.

When tracking your actual expenses (on a weekly or monthly basis) you need to always consider:

- How did your fixed costs vary from your budget, was it caused by an increase that leads to business growth?

- Did your variable sales costs maintain their relation with your sales results?

- Did your costs vary in timing or where they brought forward or delayed?

- What changes in costs or spending habits were caused by suppliers? Did payment terms, prices or policies change?

Your company's Gross Profit

Once you have analyzed your income and outcome performance, you will need to determine one of the key financial indicators for running your business.

To calculate your gross profits you need to apply the following formula:

Your Period Sales – Same Period Cost of Goods Sold = Gross Profit

This is where it is very important to know the difference and variation of variable and fixed costs.

Fixed costs will be repeated and constant in your operation, and they might include:

- Payroll

- Payroll Taxes

- Insurance

- Gas and travel expenses

- Professional and service fees

- Rent or Mortgage

- Utilities

- Office expenses like supplies, cleaning services, etc.

Variable costs will change based on the amount of products or services made, and are a direct result of producing a product or providing a service.

These costs may include:

- Distribution costs, freight.

- Materials used

- Production Equipment

- Packaging expenses

- Additional personnel required to produce

- Utilities for plant or warehouse, or storage services

- Commissions or performance bonuses

Your fixed expenses will be defined like your operating expenses.

The variable costs will be defined as your cost of goods sold.

To calculate your gross profit you will need the actual money amounts to put into the formula, but what we are seeking as gross profit will be important to be handled as a percentage. This will allow you to calculate how profitable your company is and the trends in a period.

It is VERY IMPORTANT to understand that your company can get in financial trouble if your gross profit increases but your gross profit margin declines.

We already defined how to calculate the gross profit. Now let's take a look at the gross profit margin.

The gross profit margin will be calculated by dividing your gross profit (money amount) by your sales amount.

Gross Profit / Sales = Gross Profit Margin (%)

Once you have established what your gross margin is, you can evaluate your overall company's performance and if the results you have obtained are taking you on the right track. If you are not satisfied with the results, there are two viable options to improve your margin.

You can increase the prices of your products and/or services or you can reduce the costs involved with producing them.

This is not as simple as it sounds, there are factors that can be involved that can do more harm than good to your company. For example, if you increase the prices, you run the risk of costumers seeking other options, causing your sales to drop. And if they suffer too much, you may not be able to cover your operating expenses.

Increasing your prices, please consider:
- Evaluating Inflation rates

- Have your prices remained static for long periods, several years? You are paying more to suppliers, more salaries, everything has increased but you have not increased your pricing?

- Analyzing your competition

  - Will you be much more expensive than your competition? Will you be the same price or still slightly lower? Does your product or service distinguish itself from the competition and is premium compared to them? Are you an economical substitute to one of their products?

- Supply and Demand for products you produce

  - If you order more from suppliers to reduce pricing of costs, can you move that inventory?

  - If you try to increase volume in units, can you supply without affecting your deliveries, client service, etc.?

  - If you go on sale to attract customers, can you deliver if a lot of them answer to your sales? Or will you fall short and probably anger customers?

If you make a decision regarding your prices, be sure to analyze everything you can before you make a change. A small business has to stay competitive, and most companies relate competitiveness with the price of their products and services. This can be accurate, but there are differences between a small businesses trying to compete with big companies. Just to start, the big companies have advantages regarding costs of products with suppliers, and many other factors. But small businesses can be agile and provide a better service, if your company can establish why they are different and better, and the costumer understands it, then you can be able to vary your prices.

*Remember, the price of a product is defined by what the customer is **WILLING TO PAY**, not necessarily by the costs to produce it and operate.*

Lowering your costs:

Another option for your company to increase the profit margin, is to evaluate your costs, and find a way to reduce them without affecting quantities and more importantly quality. There are ways you can decrease your costs in materials, negotiating with suppliers, buying in larger quantities, or finding a strategy to make your products in a more efficient manner.

When evaluating your costs in manufacturing, you have to consider your suppliers, and discuss with them the ways you can reduce material costs. Other options can be to seek different suppliers, ones that could offer you a better price or conditions without risking the quality of your end products.

There are other factors you can consider when analyzing cost reduction strategies, no mattering if you manufacture, wholesale, retail or provide a service, you always have to be on the lookout for ways to become more efficient. And if you find better options, just make sure you are in balance with the quality you want to provide to your customers.

Make sure you never confuse gross profit with markup. That is a common mistake because they pretty much deal with the same variables. You need to be clear that gross profit is a percentage of the selling price, and markup is a percentage of the cost.

Markup formula:

(Selling price − Cost to produce) / Cost to produce = Markup percentage

Example:

Year 1: (3 million − 2.5 million) / 2.5 million = 20%

Year 2: (2.8million − 2.1 million)/2.1 million = 33%

As you can see the comparison, year one, the sales were higher that year two, but the costs too, so even though the income was reduced, the profits increased significantly.

It is a simple process to calculate this for an entire year of business, using the markup tool in every quote to evaluate your price and potential profit, can become essential.

If you evaluate your previous years and establish the markup, it can allow you to establish control points for your success. If you can do this for individual products, quotes or projects going forward you can make a difference in your results and the profits of your operation.

CHAPTER 7

Pricing your Products or Services

A key aspect of establishing a price is not what the product or service is costing you, but what the customer is willing to pay for it. If you are able to establish this and set your prices correctly, it can increase your profits almost instantly.

A lot of companies work out their pricing system based on what each product or service will cost and once that is established, then add a reasonable markup. This is known as cost plus pricing.

That is a very common practice, but if not given serious thought and analysis from the early stages of your plan, it can become an anchor for your company and limit the growth in the future. This happens when unknown variable arise in different business scenarios and the manager or owner are forced to decide what to do to stay competitive. These variables can include a raise in costs, like hiring personnel, rent increase, pricing from suppliers and other factors that will influence your profit margins in the long run. This can cause a product or service to become not profitable, but you cannot change it because it is a customer favorite. And if you increase it, they might seek business elsewhere.

Make sure you invest a lot of time analyzing the prices of your products or services, if you dedicate time to your price structure, and try to factor all the variables, it will pay big later on.

Pricing can be based on three key elements:

1. Value: What is your service or product worth to your costumers?

We already know how to establish the cost of your product or service, and the price has the objective of establishing your financial reward for providing it.

The value is defined by what the customer thinks your product or service is worth.

For example: A repair man can come and help you in your home to fix something, and he can spend 10 dollars to get there, 4 or 5 for materials and the time he spends there fixing it. A couple of hours ($10 per hour). He could easily charge 35 dollars and it could be a fair price for him. But, if he can make it early, or late in the afternoon, or at night, and be responsible and punctual and guarantee his service for 3 months, would you mind if he charges you $.100.00? (That is your perspective as a costumer and how you assign the value)

Another repair man could quote you $45.00 but he can only get there between 8 and 5 and not an exact time because he has an open schedule, and he does not guarantee his work.

You see the difference? How the value of your service or product can influence the price?

Value based pricing is generally more applicable for the service industry, food industry, and other types of industries that can distinguish themselves from competitors with key factors that include high levels of service and quality.

Product pricing, like retail and others, usually are defined in a cost plus basis, but depending on your company, the competition and the services you can provide with a purchase or post purchase, you can add value to your products and with that, justify the pricing change.

In both cases you need to understand thoroughly your costs and your competition.

DISCOUNTS:

BE CAREFUL- Companies usually use this strategy to attract more customers, or to move inventory, and it can lead customers to ask, is his margin so high he can discount that much, that often?

If discounts are part of your strategy, you have to be sure you are sure of why you need to do it and if it will accomplish any of the following:

- Get clients to spend big with bulk discounts. Getting them to place bigger orders so they can save.

- If you have analyzed your budgets and cash flow and you have established quiet periods for your business, you can strategically place discounts to attract movement to your slow periods.

- Accumulative discounts, persuading clients to buy a certain brand or product and when they reach a number they can perceive benefits.

- Matching the competition by offering the same product at the same or a bit less price. (ONLY if it makes sense in your operation, sometimes big companies lose money on certain products to force small businesses to lower the prices and trying to compete. MAKE SURE you understand your competition and if it is reasonable, try it for short periods)

- Slow Inventory: If you have products that are taking up space in storage and warehouse, you can improve your cash flow with clearance sales. You can sell them at huge discounts to try to get rid of them quickly. Make sure you know your inventory levels and that it is a practice you DO NOT need to apply often.

If your company needs to do clearances very often to move stock, you have a serious purchasing problem and you are buying more than you should or products you don't need.

- Cash Flow discounts: If you have costumers that have certain periods of grace to pay, you can offer them discounts if they pay in cash with the order, or a different percentage if they pay sooner. For example: If you pay as soon as you get the product or place the order you can get a 5% discount, if you pay within 30 days of the invoice being issued, you can get a 2% discount. This can help you get paid sooner.

2. Costs: what does it cost you to provide that service or produce that product?

A cost structure is essential to provide you with a base for what you need to charge for a service or product. But a cost structure will not necessarily tell you what you should or can charge.

We have already established that costs will be divided into variable and fixed. And as long as the price you establish and if you meet your sales goals cover the variable costs, each sale you make will contribute toward your fixed costs and making profits.

For example:

You order 1000 shirts + 1000 pants + 1000 pair of shoes for your store. (All of the cost the same)

The variable costs of those products including the purchase of inventory, warehouse fees, taxes in imports and all the variable costs add up to 50,000 dollars.

Your fixed costs for the period when you plan to sell those products (let's say a year) are 100,000 dollars.

Total number of products = 3,000

Variable costs= $50,000

Variable Cost of products = $.16.67 per unit to cover the variable costs. This is the contribution each unit has to make to cover their variable costs.

Fixed costs= $100,000

Units in stock to cover the Fixed cost= 3,000

Fixed cost of products= $33.33 per unit to contribute to cover the fixed costs of the company.

Breakeven Price for the period= Variable cost of product + fixed cost of product =

Breakeven price= $.50.00 per unit

That is the MINIMUM price you could charge to break even if you meet your sales goal and sell all 3,000 units. But at that price you are not generating profit, and if you sell less, you are losing money. This where you need to establish the starting point for your price. Your costs are covered and you want to generate profits. By selling all 3,000 at a reasonable price, with a decent margin, or if your product is worth it and your market allows it, cover your costs with less units.

3. Competition: How does your products or services compare to your competition and how do they differ in pricing.

You are aware that your competition can influence your prices, volumes and achieving your goals. If you are smart about this, you can create a strategy that allows you to become more profitable and efficient in your operation.

If you need to evaluate your competition and its pricing, you can use the traditional strategy of asking from a third party quote. Having someone ask for a quotation from them for different quantities and conditions and with that you can learn their pricing strategies and compare them to yours.

If you gather accurate information on pricing from competitors, you have to evaluate if you need to make changes to your own prices. There are risks involved if you set your prices too low, or if you increase them without a viable reason to do so.

If you reduce them significantly you can attract customers, but at the same time you can reduce your profits significantly if the number of client's doesn't increase the volume to reduce your costs and maintain the level of profitability. Additionally, if you change them down, and your customers don't increase, if you try to raise them again, you can lose clients.

If you raise prices without a valid reason for doing so, you will force your customers to seek options. And if they find a good one, they might go to another supplier. Price increases in products have to be justified by a clear difference between you and your customers.

Whenever you are considering changing your prices, your competition can set a benchmark. But you need to be careful when you compare yourself to other companies. There are prices you can compete with, and other situations that will never allow you to be competitive when regards to pricing.

If you try to compare yourself with industry giant, like retailers, supermarkets, or chains, there is a major factor you need to consider, their costs and volumes are completely different than yours. This means your margins are going to differ from theirs.

Another variable to consider is that major companies can decrease prices in certain products to flush out the competition. They can even lose money on a specific product to force small businesses to discount their prices, and put their profits and success at risk. This strategy is something that a big company can endure, but for a small business, it is hard to compete when your margins and profits can put your company at risk if one product underperforms.

If you find a product or service that your competition provides for a lot less you have to evaluate your costs and determine if there is something you can do on your end to be more competitive. If you cannot reduce pricing, you need to have a reason to justify the difference in pricing, and be clear about it with your clients.

For example, if you sell fridges or TV's, your prices competing with big chains can be very different, but if you are more expensive you can be clear about your levels of service, free installation, discount coupon in future purchases, or something to make the client feel like the decision to buy with you was better than going to a giant store and saving a few dollars.

PRICING STRATEGIES CONSIDERATIONS

Having discussed several important aspects of a pricing structure, if you feel your company has to evaluate its current pricing strategy, then please take the following considerations:

- Marking Up your Prices

    - A traditional method of pricing is the Cost – Plus Strategy, this one is usually based on the cost of your products and the desired profit you want, and/or the percentage used by your competitor's prices based and compared to your costs to determine if it can be less or more profitable.

    - This is usually a percentage that can vary depending on your industry, location, costs, etc.

- Before you consider increasing or decreasing your prices, EVALUATE AND ANALYZE ALL your costs.

    - If you compare your pricing to other competitors, determine if it is caused by your costs or if there is something your competition is doing that you need to do.

    - Always focus on costs before making a decision to risk your desired profits.

- Know your Industry:

    - The different products and services can vary in pricing according to the industry.

        - If your company supplies different industries, make sure you are aware of the difference in each industry and that you are respectful of the margins.

        - Some companies can be very competitive in a product or service, but be completely off in another product because they apply the same margins to all their catalog. For example, they can apply a 35% margin across the board, when some products can have a larger margin or others need to have a lower one.

YOUR PROFIT MARGINS

Simply put, your margins will indicate the percentage of profits your company will make after applying the mark up.

If you buy a product for $.50.00 dollars and mark it up by 50%, selling it for $.75.00, the margin is 33.33% ((The value of the markup / selling price) x 100)

This result will give you a great indicator of the performance of each of your products and services, and with that evaluate the areas of your business where you can become more profitable.

When evaluating your margins always be careful that products or services that have low margins and low volume of sales, do not occupy a lot of space in storage or time in your business. Make sure you do not put at risk sales or resources for your high margin products or services.

Pricing based on Value

This pricing strategy is based on what your customers are willing to pay, not only based on your costs.

This strategy has to be supported by something that sets you apart from the competition, an aspect of your product or service that adds value to what you offer that is similar to your competition.

Small business companies have a tendency to try and compete with big companies, and most of the focus is based on pricing. Trying to offer the same prices as the corporations or chains that have a different cost and margin structure. This can be a major risk if you are not aware of your own costs and if you are willing to sacrifice profits just to increase the volume. Sometimes it is more than small companies can handle.

But at the same time, if you consider value based pricing, it is an opportunity to figure out how you stand out in the industry, what added services or aspects of your business can add value compared to your competition. And with that, you can justify a higher price for your products and services.

If you need to evaluate value based pricing you have to consider

- Brand: Do you offer a similar product to your competition but your brand is higher in quality? If your customer understands this and is willing to accept your product as a better one, you should communicate this clearly to your clients. Your brand marketing strategy has to be oriented to differentiating your product from the rest.

- Latest trends and exclusiveness: Do you offer products or services not yet available in other stores or competitors? Some customers are willing to spend more for premium and exclusive and new products or services. If you are the only company providing that product or service, then you have no problem with setting the pricing structure that is convenient and profitable for your company.

- Convenience: Do you go above and beyond when delivering a product or service? Do you provide a difference maker that your competitors do not offer? This strategy is well suited for small businesses, since they have the ability to provide a more personal service, they can figure out specific needs of the customer and if they are able to provide something that makes them feel like they are paying more, but getting a better deal. (Example, free installation, free delivery, etc.)

Value based pricing is something that can provide your company with increase profits, but be careful not to marginalize your customers and end up selling fewer products with higher margins. And ending up with the same income but less clients.

Pricing Flexibility:

Many department stores have a pricing strategy that differs according to season, type of product, volumes, rotation and several other factors that are designed to attract customers when they want or need.

Does your company have different margins for different products? Or do you base your prices in one overall margin and apply it across the board to all your products and services?

Being flexible in your pricing can allow you to increase inventory rotation and become more profitable. As well as managing your cash flow more efficiently and based on what you need to accomplish.

To determine your flexibility you may need to consider:

- Products might need to have the higher margins:

    - Products or services that have a slow inventory rotation

        - The variable costs of these products is a lot higher since they require more controls in your operation to make sure they are available.

    - Products that take a lot of space in the warehouse

        - The rent you pay on storage or warehouse services will increase based on the space the products take up and the time it takes them to exit the warehouse.

    - Products with high distribution costs

        - Depending on what you offer, some products might require additional investments to make them available to your final client. These variable costs will vary according to the type of product and would need to be considered when pricing.

    - Products with low unit costs

        - The lower your costs, the more room for margin you have. If you know your competition and it´s prices you want to maximize profits and stay competitive.

    - Seasonal products that are available for a limited time

- Knowing you will invest in a specific product or service that will be available on limited basis, you can try and maximize your profits. And if at the end of the season you are left with some stock, a clearance sale can help you cover the costs of the investment. (For example Christmas decorations, they sell at premium prices during Holliday season and at the end they go on clearance)

- Premium products or services. (For example a handyman that charges market prices during the day to ensure a lot of appointments – but premium charges or fees for emergencies after hours when clients would be willing to pay more.

Flexible pricing is needed to help your company become more profitable and efficient. To achieve this you need to know each of your products and services, what they cost, and how much the can contribute in profits. Based on your market, your competition and any other factor that might allow you to be more competitive and more profitable. This area of pricing analysis is to help you define a strategy for each of your products and services, and establish the correct and competitive margins that will allow you to become more profitable.

Fading Opportunities

When evaluating your pricing structure you have to establish guidelines or control points for your products and services. As every company needs to be aware if they are offering products or services that will or have become obsolete.

The simplest example of this would be if you sell perishable products. The products will become worthless for you and your company if they expiration date arrives and you have not been able to sell them. This can be applied to grocery stores, or small restaurants for example.

If you are discarding certain amount of products every day, week or month, then your strategy is not suitable for those products. You either do not know your market, you are pricing your products incorrectly, or your purchases are not aligned with the reality of your operation and the results being obtained.

Just like perishable products, technology products and services and become obsolete as new models or versions become available. If you have invested in technology products and services and you offer something that gradually became obsolete, you need to find out the exact reason of why they did not sell or why they are not being well received by your customers.

If you get to the point where you have to sell the products with an extreme discount just to get them out of stock, you need to explain to yourself and your clients the reason. And your explanation has to be sensible and plausible to allow your customers to keep trusting you.

If you are not sure about your pricing strategy and how to establish the limits of what your clients would be willing to pay, always remember, aim high. You can be prepared to lower the prices if your sales goals are not being met, or if you need to improve your cash flow.

As you already know, low prices are or can be associated with the quality of the product or service. If that is your current image, then take the necessary steps to change it. And if you are a company that is about to start, DO NOT make the mistake of trying to compete based on pricing.

It is generally the other way around, big companies are usually forced to lower their prices if they cannot compete with the quality in service. Be absolutely clear on what you can offer that is better in service and overall client satisfaction if you are not able to compete in pricing. Never underprice your products or services to build up sales if it is not absolutely required.

What added value will you give to your customers?

How are you making sure you influence the buying decision so it is not based solely on pricing?

Remember: it is simpler to reduce prices than to increase them. Make sure you are applying the correct strategy on your prices.

Pricing Tactics

There are certain option you can apply to your pricing strategy that can influence customers to purchase with you instead of with your competition. These are factors additional to your cost or perceived value and it can help your company reach goals or set new objectives in your business plan or marketing plan.

Examples:

One of the most common pricing tactic known in the US is Black Friday, but many small businesses do not understand how to apply it and take advantage of this occasion.

Big chain companies use a simple strategy to make people line up or camp out in their doors for hours or nights just so they apparently save a lot of money. They create a list of loss leaders to attract new customers, but there´s a catch, they are limited in number. And customers know it, but are son excited of what they can save that they camp out and wait for hours to get the chance to save that much on a specific product.

They take computers that probably sell for $600.00 on a regular day and advertise them for $299.00 and that is a huge discount. But the fine print indicated there are only 50 available. So the client knows that and hopes he is one of the 50 to get there soon enough to save almost 300 dollars. And if he is well great, but if he is not, he will buy the next best thing, or something completely unplanned. But the mission was to get clients ready to spend in your store. And that has been achieved.

Some small businesses try to do the same and offer across the board discounts, sacrificing profits for volume. Investing in ads to get people in just with a 20% or 50% off in the pricing. But the key aspect of the advertising is to offer something completely unavailable any other time of the year. And the simple discount is being offered by everyone. But if you notice the big chains, they are offering it only in certain products, not in all. Some products even go up in Black Friday, because the clients coming in feel they saved 300 dollars in a computer, so they are willing to spend those 300 in something else. In products that have normal or even higher margins.

That is one of the most common strategies that involves:

- Odd values (something being 199.99 instead of 200)

- Loss leaders (To attract new customers)

- Pricing war (Being able to sell at much lower prices to win market share from competitors) (This is used by companies that have deep pockets)

Making Changes in your Pricing Strategy

If you consider making changes in your current pricing strategy you have to be aware of all the variables that can be involved and the repercussions that might arise from changes.

First of all you need to be completely sure about your costs and margins, and how they can compare to your competition. Once this information has been thoroughly analyzed you can start evaluating the changes and taking the necessary steps to do it.

Be aware of what your customers would do, try to be as realistic as you can when thinking about it from your clients perspective. Run the numbers to simulate if you can increase your profits even if your volumes decrease with the price increase. If possible, talk to customers that you have a relationship with and gain their perspective before making the change.

If you are able to present the reasoning for the price change, be sure to market yourself as well. You need to explain the reasoning on the prices and make sure your client understands why it would or is better buying from you rather than with a competitor. This is where you need to have the elements to back up your cost in relation to the high quality of prior and after sales service.

You can damage a relationship with a client if there is no good reasoning in your high prices, and even though the customer might have some or no options, if you are not able to demonstrate and have the strategy to continue delivering that added value, your customer relationship might suffer significantly.

For this analysis in your business plan or operation, you need to have full control of your variable costs, or have the ability to modify and improve them with your suppliers. Either by seeking new options in suppliers or discussing a price drop from them if certain conditions are met that are beneficial for both companies.

Fixed costs are also an element in pricing strategies. Your growth plans can be tied down with reaching your goals. And if you are not realistic, and fail to meet them, your fixed costs could increase and put your profit margins at risk. Ruining your pricing strategy if not considered carefully.

Another variable to include in your analysis is the performance of your product mix. That will be established when you analyze each product separately, how their variable costs differ and what they contribute to your fixed costs and margins. If you determine a product has a small margin, it can't be increased because of market conditions, it takes up a lot of space in the warehouse, or a lot of time in the sales process, you might consider eliminating that product from your mix.

CHAPTER 8
Business Plan Basics

Why do companies place such importance into a business plan? Well, the creation of a business plan will allow any company to develop a roadmap to where they want to go and more importantly, how they are going to get there.

You can have great ideas, but without planning, the implementation of any idea or the development of any good product can get lost. And especially in a small business, as this can be a time consuming process and small business owners can lack motivation in investing so much time in a plan that they know will probably change over time. Or in dedicating themselves in something that will not immediately produce them income.

A good business plan will add value to your company, and in the long run will allow your company to achieve goals in a more efficient manner. Putting your concepts and ideas in a plan will allow you to learn about your market, competitors, and prepare your company for the changes needed to succeed.

Having a business plan can give your company a lot of benefits, it can help you:

-   Verify if an idea can be successful

-   Give you a clear perspective of your industry

-   Identify the opportunities and threats in your market

-   Develop a company document that can introduce you to potential employees, vendors, suppliers.

-   Establish benchmarks to evaluate and monitor performance

-   Analyze and evaluate your competition and their strategies

-   Explain clearly your products and services

-   Justify your marketing strategy

- Create a guidelines document to help you keep your focus

- Define clearly your mission, vision and values

- Understand your financial structure and needs

Not having a business plan will increase the risks and uncertainties in your business. You can put your company in financial trouble, lose customers because of poor service, missing your sales projections because you are not clear about your customer's needs and you can become overwhelmed with the options an ever changing business will face.

With all the topics covered previously, you will have no trouble developing a business plan for your company. This document will be a guideline for your company, and you will be able to change it and modify it as you need. A business plan will outline the road you want to take to achieve your goals and objectives for the next 3 to 5 years.

Business Plan Structure:

1- Executive Summary

Considered one of the most important parts of a business plan, this section of the document will introduce your company, your idea and where you want to take it. And more importantly, why you will be successful. Your objective in this part of the plan is to explain your strengths and overall plan. This part of the business plan can change as you advance in every section, and you might even want to leave it for last.

If your company is already running you need to include the following information in the executive summary:

- Mission Statement: Where you explain what your company is all about.

- Company Information: This outlines a brief description on who founded the company, the legal structure, when it was established, the founders' roles, the number of employees and the different locations you operate.

- Growth History: Here you can detail the examples of how your company has grown, you can include graphs and charts to detail your financial or market achievements.

- Services or Products: Provide a description of the products and/or services your company provides. The market you will serve and your competitive advantages.

- Financial Information: Here you can outline the information about your current investors or bank as well as sales, profits, cash flow, etc.

- Future Plans: Detail where you want to take your company.

Try to be concise with your information. The mission statement will be a couple of sentences or a paragraph, and the rest of your Executive summary can be covered in one page if you are accurate with and brief with your information.

If you are a company that is on the starting phase you will find it difficult to gather and present as much information as if you were already operating. In such case you will want to present all the experience and decisions that led to start the company. You need to prove that you know the market, the product and the customers. With this information you will have to explain how you plan to succeed.

2- Business Description

Usually this is the first part of the Business plan you want to address. You will use this part to explain the goal of your company and the unique proposition it will present.

It is key to start this section with a description of the industry, presenting its current state and what you expect the future outcome to be. It is very important that you present accurate and reliable data regarding the industry and market. If you are seeking potential investors you need to present figures that are reliable and trustworthy. You cannot assume or speculate.

The structure and nature of your business and the needs you will be satisfying will have to be detailed and explained. How you will operate (Wholesale, retail, food service, technology, etc.) and how your products or services will meet the market needs and how you have a competitive advantage that will lead you to be a success.

You can list the key personnel you will or currently have that will allow you to bring value to your specific customers or consumers, organizations or businesses that your company will or currently serve.

How will you profit? You don´t need to write 20 pages on how you will be profitable. But you have to be specific on how you will give your company a competitive edge, why you will be better compared to your competition and why your market proposition will be unique. (Higher quality products, better service, additional products, delivery services, etc.)

Make sure you explain all variables that will influence your success, like key personnel, training, location, equipment and any other element that might influence why you will succeed.

If you are seeking investment you have to structure the document for financial purpose, and explain why the additional equity or debt money will increase your profit structure. You need to demonstrate how you will use that money to expand or generate additional profits. If for example you are expanding and require additional funds for another location, you have to specify where and why that location will influence your success.

This section of your business plan can be a few pages or a few paragraphs, it all comes down to your objectives and the complexity of the business. Always try to be short but effective when describing your business and its purpose.

3- Market Analysis

After the company description you will have to present in detail the market knowledge you possess and all the research you have done about your industry.

Current information on your industry and Future Outlook: Here you will need to gather all the data regarding your industry, like the size, the historical growth, life cycle, projected growth and any other trends and characteristics you find relevant.

Your Target Market: A lot of small companies make the mistake of trying to appeal to everyone. In this part of your analysis you will have to define the distinguishing characteristics of your consumers. The critical needs the have and how they are currently being met or not met. You need to be specific regarding location, demographics and everything relevant with your potential customers.

Additional to the size of your market what other data can you present? How much do they spend? Can you assign a value to your market and can you forecast the growth?

(There are free government resources that can assist you with this and can help you build the profile for your market. There will be 3 key factors in this research you can get from government websites: Economic Indicators – Employment Statistics – Income and Earnings) (You can also seek groups and institutions that work within the industry that can help you with data)

Market Share – Pricing and Targets: Here you have to present your defined pricing structure, your profit margins and the pricing strategy you plan to implement. Be sure you include any tests or research you completed and after a set period of time, how much of the market share you plan to control if you achieve your goals.

Competitive Analysis and Restrictions: Based on the types of products or services you provide you need to identify your competition and how they compare to you. With this information you need to structure the competition landscape that compares all the companies in your list with the participation they have in the market. You need to answer how the Market share is distributed at the moment, what are your strengths and weaknesses as well as your competitors. Additionally you need to identify if there are any risks that may limit your company as it enters the market, and if you will pursue an important target market from your competitors. Are there any other companies that can influence your success? Are there barriers that can limit your results? (Investment amounts, evolving technology, limited access to adequate personnel, etc.)

Are there any customer, government or any other requirements that may impact on an operational or cost level? You need to present any requirements that might pose a risk for your business performance or growth.

4- Organization and Management

After describing in detail your Market Analysis you have to present the section of Organizational and Management with details about the ownership of the company, the profiles of your employees and the qualifications of each member of your team. (Including the Board of Directors)

This section is with de objective of defining who does what in your company. The background of your employees, their responsibilities, their salaries and benefits and the incentives package you have established for your organization.

An organizational chart with a description of each of the positions within your company (Does not matter if it is only 2 people) will provide you with the knowledge of what is being exactly done by each of your team members. And more specifically, what is expected from them. This will also help you ensure that you are not repeating parts of your business process and your organization is efficient and effective.

Regarding the ownership information you should incorporate the name of everyone, their percentage and form of ownership, their involvement within the operations, if they have outstanding equity and what they bring to the table. Either with equity, skills, knowledge, etc. Try to incorporate all the details of their track record and their unique experience and skills if possible.

Everyone in your company has to compliment your own skills. You have to be clear about your own skills and limitations, and describing them in this section will allow you to highlight how each team member can contribute to your company's success.

Your Organizational Structure will be an essential element within your business plan because it will provide a base for your operating expenses. Most companies vary in the type of organizational structure but some of the common areas they can always be considered are marketing and sales, production and administration.

Your company may be different, and you will have to structure this area and list your own requirements and goals. For this you will need to organize your list of tasks in a broad classification and assign these tasks to a specific department that will allow an efficient line of communication between customer, staff and management.

As you evaluate these tasks you will be able to determine the type of employee required to perform each task and establish the function of how it will relate to generating income or expense within the company. Additionally you have to set the limits of your structure, considering your overall goals and the number of employees you will need to reach them. For example, how many customers can an employee serve? If your goal in a department is to serve 1,500 clients and each employee can realistically serve 150, they you would require 10 employees for a specific department.

All this information will help you set, verify and quantify your goals. As well as what you require to reach them. Please note that this section of the business plan can go into as much detail as possible as it will assist you in establishing costs and monitor performance.

5- Service or Product Description

What will you be providing as a product or service? What will your benefits be for potential or current customers? In this section you need to focus on why your product will be better and different.

Be specific about the benefits of your product or service, try to describe how it will satisfy customers' needs and detail any advantages you can clearly establish over your competition. In this area you want to include information about your product's lifecycle, if there are any factors that can influence the need for this product or service in the future and how you plan to adapt if such changes arise.

6- Marketing and Sales

This part of the business plan has to detail your sales and marketing strategy. What tasks will you perform to attract and retain customers, how will you make sure they come back to you for business?

In this section you will want to define your sales strategy, and how it is aligned with your marketing strategy. The main idea is to detail the tactics you will use to drive sales and gain customer loyalty.

A marketing and sales strategy will vary specifically to what you want to achieve. The goals you set have to be attainable and realistic to your market conditions, resources, personnel and your capacity. For this segment of the business plan you will want to describe how you will penetrate the market, how you will build a growth strategy that will allow you to increase the number of customers, profits, personnel and any other aspect of your business related to growth.

It is imperative you communicate two key elements of your sales and marketing strategy, what type of customer will you be reaching, and how will you achieve an efficient communication with them. How will you reach them to attract new potential customers and how will you maintain your current ones in the loop and provide them with great service.

A sales strategy will have to be structured specifically for your sales force. Will you use internal or independent representatives? How big will your sales force be? After defining that you will have to break down the activities within your sales force, what aspects of the sales process will depend on the sales force and what tasks will be responsibility of other departments? You need to set priorities on how you will reach the customer, how you will get them to see your product or service and how you will obtain the business. And after that, how will you get them to come back?

An effective sales and marketing strategy will allow you to clearly understand how you plan to sell your product or service, how you will communicate with the customer to do so, and how to get them to come back again and again.

7- Financial Projections

After you have analyzed the market and defined your business goals and objectives you need to evaluate the resources needed to back up your business plan.

If you are established business you need to include your historical data related to your performance. This will allow you to prove to any potential investors or banks of your history, growth and how you manage your resources. Every year you need to update and include your latest financial statements.

Income Statement: This report will demonstrate the ability of your company to generate cash. It will be a performance indicator that reflects when sales income is generated and when expenses are incurred.

Cash Flow Statement: This statement will detail how much and when money will be generated, available and when it will be needed to fulfill your obligations. The result will be a profit or loss at the end of a period.

Balance Sheet: A summary of all the financial information broken down into three areas, Assets, Liabilities and Equity. Unlike previous statements this is generated only on an annual basis.

Usually you can go up to five years back and include your cash flow statements, your balance sheets and income statements. This will allow you to evaluate your performance and compare it to your current results. As well as helping you define new objectives and goals.

If you are requesting funds, or trying to establish the resources you need to start operating you have to project your results for future periods of time. You will have to forecast your results and include simulated cash flows, balance sheets and income statements.

If you are planning for the future, either with an established company or a business idea you need funding to implement, you will have to establish first year projections per quarter or month. Being specific of what you want to achieve, how you will spend the money, loan or income generated by your sales.

Historical and prospective financial information will allow you to determine where you have been, where you can improve and where you want to go. You can add graphs and trend analysis to highlight areas of importance or relevance.

A lot of small companies do not believe that a business plan is only needed if you are going to get a loan or investor, and because of that they do not consider it relevant or needed.

It is important for a small business owner that this will allow you to be better prepared, evaluate your performance and lead you to grow and adapt to achieve any goals you set for your company. Let's be clear about something, a business plan will help you think or even define your strategy. It will allow you to establish what is unique about your company, its product or services. After doing that you will be able to think about who you want to sell it to, and how to do so.

The business plan can be very simple, an internal document that can serve you as a guide of what your vision is, what you have accomplished so far and where you want your company to be in 3 to 5 years.

If you create a business plan, or a simplified version of it; make sure you include deadlines, dates and what you want to happen. Make a list that you can manage and assign responsibility to specific team members of the tasks that need to be achieved. Make sure you establish a calendar to review your plan, the list and what you have been able to achieve.

CHAPTER 9

Small Business Marketing Essentials

Marketing is the business strategy designed to be the link between what your business is selling and what your costumers are buying. It is talking WITH your costumers instead of to them.

Marketing is a cycle that starts with costumer knowledge and goes around your whole operation all the way to customer service.

Each company has completely different needs and tactics that can be implemented to create a marketing plan. However, the process, resources and time required to develop and execute an efficient marketing strategy is based on the same principles.

It does not make a difference if a marketing strategy is designed for an individual starting a company by himself or for a multinational company that sells billions and can spend millions in a marketing campaign. The steps needed to build a marketing program that can help you become strong company that can gain and keep clients is going to involve the same variables no matter the size of a company.

Step 1: Research Phase for Product – Service – Customer – Competition

You need to investigate and get to know EVERYTHING you can about your customers, your product, and the market you will serve, the competitors you will face.

Step 2: Develop the product

With the information gathered in step 1, you will be able to evaluate if your price, presentation and strategies for delivery and distribution will meet your customer's necessities, your markets conditions and allow you to be competitive. Compare your product design, presentation, and everything you need to stand out from the crowd. This can influence your costs and may determine if you get more or less sales.

Step 3: Distribution

This can determine additional costs for your products, and it can become a competitive advantage if you figure out options to become more cost and time efficient. What services does your competition offer that add value? How can you improve them without varying your costs significantly?

Step 4: Establish your Pricing Strategy

Your goal is to be competitive and profitable. Once you know your market, customer and competition, you can compare the data with your costs and determine what best pricing strategy can suit you to maximize your profits and be competitive.

Step 5: Promotions – Ad Campaigns – Public relations

The objective of this step is to communicate with potential or current customers. What message do you want to deliver to your current customers so they can return in a shorter time period? What message do you need to get to potential customers to make them consider you as an option? Once the messages are established and clear, how can you transmit it to them efficiently and in a cost suited with your budget capacity?

Step 6: Sales Process

Client interaction – this is a vital part of your marketing strategy. This is where you can gather information about your customers' needs and if you are delivering a quality product or service. This is continuous research that will allow you to gain knowledge about the results of your previous steps. Pay attention and gather information that will help you change the strategies and become better every time you develop a plan.

Step 7: Customer Service

As soon as the sales process ends, the customer service step begins. This step is critical for return business, client referrals and keeping clients happy. The customer service step is where you build relationships and get personal. As a small business you have a huge advantage over large corporations and chains. Your communication channel is a lot closer if not immediate with the customer. This allows you to react, prepare and provide a better service than any of the big chains.

Another key aspect that can put you in a better position for a marketing strategy is the fact that as a small business you can get a lot closer and more personal with your customers.

Some key tips you can use to establish your marketing can be focused on:

- **Your Market:** Having a grasp and clear understanding of your market, the trends, changes, opportunities and consumer demographics, will provide you with the option of narrowing the base of your consumers. Knowing exactly who you want to reach, where they are located and how many there are within your service area, will allow you to communicate with them with an effective and direct message. You can begin with getting to know the current customers you have, gathering information about their age, where they live, what they like and all the data that would allow you to help them value your company and make them want to come back.

- **The customer:** If you know your market, your clients and their needs, and how you are able to satisfy those needs, you will be able to develop a strategy that can help you gain advantage over your competition.

  A strategy to get them into your company is key, but getting them to return is as, if not more, important.

- **Be clear about your objectives:** A marketing plan or strategy cannot be vague and general. You need to be able to quantify results and evaluate performance. Get a clear goal in mind, and a recommendation would be to develop a strategy to gain new customers and a different strategy to retain the current ones. Getting them to come back is essential for your success and stability, new business will allow you to grow.

- **Budget:** Understand that any investment hast to generate a return. You cannot spend money without knowing exactly what it will generate in return. But to start, you have to assign the resources needed to execute that plan.

- **Invest in your Brand:** It can be your own name if you are starting by yourself to promote a product or service. But if you establish a business plan and want to develop and create a brand, please be aware that it is not only a logo, it will be something that has to stand out from the crowd. You will get one chance to get it right, make sure you think it through and in the long term.

- *Understand Marketing and Advertising:* Be absolutely sure that you are not wasting your time and money on investments that you cannot justify or quantify. One of the biggest mistakes small companies make is assigning budgets and spending a lot of money on ad campaigns to try and compete with big companies. Advertising in a part of a strategy, it cannot be the only marketing strategy. There are many different ways you can market your company without spending a lot of money.

- *Goals and Targets:* If you cannot measure results, and make sure that what you are doing is generating new business or improving your numbers, then it will be pointless to invest in a campaign or a marketing strategy that you cannot quantify. Set your goals in terms of revenue, profit and number of new sales. A strategy to acquire new business will give you the opportunity, it will generate new inquiries, but it will be your responsibility to close those deals.

- *The 4 P's of Marketing:* Product – Pricing – Placement and Promotions Understand each of them clearly before you develop a plan and execute it with clear goals and objectives.

- DO NOT develop a strategy if you cannot follow through. If you invest in a website, be sure to update it frequently, if you decide to venture into social networks, assign the resources needed to manage it properly and respond promptly to customer inquiries. A lot of companies create a FB page but do not pay attention to it, same with a website. Remember these are communication channels, and if you cannot manage them properly, it is better not to have them.

You need to establish a schedule of events that will help your company get promoted, and make sure your entire team is involved and that they pitch ideas on how you can improve or create a plan. After you develop a strategy or plan you need to track progress throughout the year. Schedule meetings to evaluate your performance and results. Pick measurable objectives, you need to have the ability to monitor your progress and adjust if needed.

Getting Organized

After evaluating every area of your company, establishing your financial indicators and your company goals we reach the most important aspect of the course, the follow up.

If you start to make changes but do not supervise, track and monitor them frequently, you are destined to repeat mistakes and limit your ability to change and improve.

If you want your business to succeed, the first step is to be ready, and we have covered a lot of important aspects to help you in that area within the course. Once you are confident about every area in your company, you need to plan, execute and follow up. And you, as the owner, are the key aspect of this task.

If YOU do not get organized, you cannot expect your employees to meet your goals and needs. As we discussed earlier, you have to lead by example. If you are having issues with time management, a task list can assist you with the day to day tasks you have to do.

One of my recommendations would be to structure your areas and the information that each one generates. These are the following areas you have to organize and supervise: (Tasks may go from daily, weekly, bi weekly, monthly, quarterly, semester or yearly.)

- **Business Planning:** Set time at least once a month or once a quarter to revise the results and compare it to your projections. If you are not on top of your goals, you will not be able to adapt if changes are needed. Meet with your company managers to discuss the results and evaluate strategy.

- **Sales and Marketing:** Once or twice a month you should be evaluating the outcome of your sales and marketing efforts. What products or services are selling at high levels? Which ones are underperforming? Each of your sales reps, or managers has to report their results, pipeline and prospects. Your marketing strategies have to be quantifiable and you need to measure if that is paying off.

- **Financials:** Your Profit and Loss Statements, the Balance Sheets and all your financial indicators will give you the information you need to influence better decision making. You evaluation of each of the expenses and the income generated by your sales has to be clearly understood to see if you can correct your strategies, improve or grow.

- **Legal:** Make sure your contracts, corporate documents and intellectual property are in order. At the same time make sure your permits are up to date and if there have been changes or updates to regulations, taxes, etc.

- **Human Resources:** Evaluate results, talk to your employees, set time to gather information about your internal client. Review your Payroll, benefits and any other plans you need to supervise or execute with your employees.

- **Products and Services:** KNOW everything about your products and services, investigate your competition every certain time to see if they have made changes. (Part of your business plan revision) Revise the price structure, have your costs increased or decreased? Are there substitutes available, how are your inventory levels and rotation?

- **YOUR CUSTOMER:** gather data about traffic, consumption levels, preferred products or services, service levels, customer claims, reviews, and if possible do a random survey to evaluate your company and service from their perspective.

There are certain checklists you can establish after finishing this course, but the most important areas you need to supervise frequently are:

What an owner should always know:

On a Daily Basis:

- Bank funds, what comes in and what will go out on the day. (NEVER mix personal finances into business accounts)

- Cash on hand

- Daily summary of sales – How much, where it came from and method of payment received (Cash – check – Credit Card, deposit, etc.)

On a Weekly Basis:

- Accounts payable for next week

- Accounts receivable (To evaluate customers and improve payment times)

- Payroll

- Taxes and reports

- Bank balances

- Inventory reports

- Sales meeting with reports and updates from entire team

On a Monthly Basis:

- Profit and Loss statement for the month available, set a timeline for when you should receive it.

- Balance Sheet

- Bank Statement and reconciles (Make sure your records match your bank balances)

- Accounts receivable report

- Taxes

- Sales report and results from each member of the team (Evaluate performance)

- Purchases and Expenses report

- Inventory report, slow moving inventory indicators, dead stock, new stock ordered (so you can plan payment).

- Marketing Meeting to set promotions, evaluate promotion results, etc.

- Cash flow comparison (From projected in your budget to the actual results)

- Key performance indicators Evaluation – How did you do compared to your goals? How many clients? How much income per client, etc.

It is IMPERATIVE that you create your personal schedule, a monthly calendar of your responsibilities. Once you define your tasks, you will be able to see how much time each one takes, if you are able to keep your schedule or if there are areas where you need assistance.

No.	TASK	JANUARY																														
		1	2	3	4	5	6	7	8	9	10	11	12	13	14	15	16	17	18	19	20	21	22	23	24	25	26	27	28	29	30	31
1	Monthly Shifts Calendar																															
2	Daily Entrance Exit Control Sheets																															
	Quarterly Sales Meeting																															
3	Inventory																															
4	Supplier evaluation																															
5	Employee Payment																															
6	Daily Sales Revision																															
7	Cash Flow Revision and Update	X	X																													
8	Daily Purchases Revision																															
9	Daily purchases monthly Report																															
10	Promotion Evaluation																															
11	Accounts Payable Report		X																													
12	Accounts Receivable Report																															
13	Daily Client Revision Report																															
14	Service Evaluation																															
15	Client Feedback																															
16	KPI Monthly Summary					X	X	X																								
17	KPI Montly Evaluation					X	X	X																								
18	Achiving																															
19	Montly Payments Calendar																															
20	Monthly Budget																															
21	Cash Flow vs. Budget									X	X																					
22	Purchases Report																															
23	Sales Report																															
24	Consolidated Monthly Sales																															
25	Consolidated Sales Analysis																															

No.	TASK	1	2	3	4	5	6	7	8	9	10	11	12	13	14	15	16	17	18	19	20	21	22	23	24	25	26	27	28	29	30

Type of report	Person Responsible	Due Date	Actual Date
Daily Sales	Ana	5th	4th
Monthly Sales	Steve		
Daily Purchases	Ana		
Monthly Purchases	Steve		
Accounts payable	Ana		
Accounts receivable	Ana		
Payments Overdue	Steve		
Cash Flow and Budget	Steve		
KPI Report	Steve		

There are many other tasks you can add to your lists, and there are simple ways to monitor you doing them. *(Excel sheet example)*

You can highlight with any color on the day you are supposedly perform the task. And if you perform it, mark an X. And this will allow you to evaluate YOUR OWN PERFORMANCE! (If you mark it on the highlighted day, you were on schedule. If you mark it any other day, you can track the days you delayed your own tasks.

Example of Tasks and the day marked are the days you are supposed to perform them.

No.	TASK	1	2	3	4	5	6	7	8
1	Monthly Shifts Calendar								
2	Daily Entrance Exit Control Sheets								
	Quarterly Sales Meeting								
3	Inventory								
4	Supplier evaluation								
5	Employee Payment								
6	Daily Sales Revision								
7	Cash Flow Revision and Update	X	X						
8	Daily Purchases Revision								
9	Daily purchases monthly Report								
10	Promotion Evaluation								
11	Accounts Payable Report		X						
12	Accounts Receivable Report								
13	Daily Client Revision Report								
14	Service Evaluation								
15	Client Feedback								
16	KPI Monthly Summary					X	X	X	
17	KPI Montly Evaluation					X	X	X	

Type of reports you need to receive every month and the person responsible.

Type of report	Person Responsible	Due Date
Daily Sales	Ana	
Monthly Sales	Steve	
Monthly Purchases	Steve	
Accounts payable	Ana	
Accounts receivable	Ana	
Payments Overdue	Steve	
Cash Flow and Budget	Steve	
KPI Report	Steve	

EXERCISES AND CHECK LISTS

Business Structure:

- Who handles your accounting and do they help you analyze your performance? List the tasks and establish what areas they can assist you with.
- Do you lead your sales team? Describe the sales process, every step. Can you manage every step of the process? Are there areas you can improve or that you require assistance?
- How big is your sales team? What have their results been? Do they study and know the market and the competition?
- What is your marketing team doing? Are you responsible of marketing on your own? Do you have a strategy?
- Have you invested in advertising campaigns without having a marketing strategy? How much?

Team Needs:

- Do you know what everybody in your company does? Could you do it yourself, be in their shoes? Why not?
- What areas and departments of your business are not performing well? Why?
- Do those areas have the right team?
- Do you know your company roles? Every position?
- How is your employee turnover? How long do they stay on average?
- Do you have employee profiles? Position profiles? What exactly does each position require? Do you know every task needed to perform well in each position?
- Are your employees delivering the results you want?
- Are several employees performing the same tasks?

Leadership:

- What kind of leader are you?
- Do you involve your employees in important decisions?
- Do you delegate?
- How is your communications with employees?
- How is your communication with customers?

- Do you have a communication structure?
- Do you offer growth opportunities to your employees? Do you offer training programs to improve?
- Do you have an employee incentive program? Have you quantified the results and is it a viable option for your company?
- Have you gone through rough times in your business? Does your leadership suffer if you are going through a difficult moment? (on a personal or professional level)
- Is your company doing great and are you losing interest or not leading properly?
- What is your organization Structure?

Information
- What information do you use to make business decisions?
- Do you have a software system to capture and organize your data? If not, what do you currently use?
- Do you know how to use the system to its maximum potential?
- What reports do you analyze every week, month, and year? Who issues the reports and is the information accurate? What is the frequency?
- Do you track employee productivity and results?
- Do you have Key Performance Indicators for your business?
- What areas of your business do you need to monitor? Do you currently monitor them?
- Do you monitor your customers? Do you have any KPI's?
- What major changes and decisions have been a result of analyzing your information?

Finance
- Are your Financial Management Skills up to date?
- Do you monitor business performance?
- How many budgets do you create for your business? List each and why are they for.
- Do you use a Cash Flow Budget? Yes / No – Why?
- Who is involved in your budget preparation?
- Do you know your variable and fixed costs? Have they changed in the last 2 years? How and why?

- Do you have a Sales Forecasts?
- Do you have a Cost Forecast?
- Has your Gross Profit increased or decreased? Compare the last 3 years.
- Has your Gross Margin increased or decreased? Compare the last 3 years.
- Have your expenses grown? Why?
- Have your expenses grown in proportion to your sales results?
- Do you have a Markup Strategy? Is it across the board for all products?
- Do you know each of your products margins and performance?
- Do you have slow moving products? How long do they take to go out of your warehouse?
- Do you have dead inventory? How much is it worth?
- Do you have a Pricing Strategy? Do you have a Pricing Structure?
- Do you give out discounts often? Why?
- Have you compared your prices to your competition? How long ago?
- Do you know your industry margins?
- Do you know your market and competition?
- Do you use Cost Plus pricing? Why?
- Could you use Value Based Pricing? Why?
- Do you know your break even pricing for all your products? (At least for your leading products)
- Are your products categorized by performance? What sells the best to the worst?
- Do you have Pricing Flexibility and do you use Pricing tactics? Is there a plan?
- Do you have a business Plan, why not?
- Do you have a Marketing Strategy? Have you invested in an advertising campaign without having a marketing plan?
- Have you been able to quantify results from your marketing efforts and advertising?
- Do you have enough time to realize ALL your responsibilities in an organized and efficient manner?
- Do you have a tasks calendar?

Tasks - Checklist:

Create your organizational structure and chart.

Create employee profiles – with all the tasks, requirements and expectations for that position.

Create YOUR employee profile – list all your tasks, requirements and expectations.

Evaluate every employee to see if they meet the employee profile requirements.

- Create a Cash Flow Budget with your mixed and variables costs. (With your actual results and data from the last period)
- Create a Sales Forecast
- Create a Costs Forecast
- Create a Cash Flow Budget with your sales and costs forecast – One for a Quarter, one for the Semester and One for the next year. (Use Most Likely / Pessimistic / Optimistic Scenarios)
- Analyze your Gross Profit and Gross Margin
- Get your Balance Sheets and compare the Gross Profit and Margin, have they increased, decreased, why? What factor influenced the variation?
- Analyze your price structure
- Do you use Cost plus Pricing or could you use Value Based Pricing? Why and how can you provide the added value to charge more?
- Do a pricing comparison with your competition, could you be profitable at their prices?
- Do a Pricing Matrix
- Create a Business Plan
- Use the seven steps to evaluate your marketing options.
- Develop a marketing strategy to RETAIN CUSTOMERS and have them come back. *Include a Budget
- Develop a marketing strategy to SEEK AND GAIN CUSTOMERS. *Include a Budget

Create employee profiles – with all the tasks, requirements and expectations for that position.

Create YOUR employee profile – list all your tasks, requirements and expectations.

Evaluate every employee to see if they meet the employee profile requirements.

THANK YOU FOR BEING AN ENTREPRENEUR AND SMALL BUSINESS OWNER

I really appreciate the time and effort you put into reading this eBook. And more importantly I hope this information was useful for you and your company or project. It is not important at what stage of the business you are in, if you are just on the planning stages, or if you are a business that has been operating for a long time.

The ideas you have developed after reading this book, please put them into action. Establish what areas if your business are in need of change, and try to set a guideline and plan to improve, or change.

Please revise the exercises and checklist, answer every question as honestly as you can and do everything the task list requires. I promise that will provide you with options and insight. It will set guidelines and with that, your probability of improving and becoming more successful will increase.

If you would like more information, or the excel files shown in the examples listed in the book. Please send me an email to:

consulting@internationalsbc.com and I will gladly assist you.

Please contact me if you would like a consulting session too. We could coordinate it through email and do it over skype.

Once again, I appreciate you purchasing this book and allowing me to help you, even if it was in a small way. It has been a privilege to share my knowledge and experience with you and I truly hope I was able to present you with options and ideas. And no matter what is going on with your business, you are already a success. The task of opening a small business is monumental, and something admirable. So no matter what happens, you are already better that a lot of individuals. And believe me, even if you have failed, that doesn't mean that you act like a failure.

And remember....

"It does not matter how many times we fall down.....what we do when we get up is the key!"

www.ingramcontent.com/pod-product-compliance
Lightning Source LLC
Chambersburg PA
CBHW051921170526
45168CB00001B/491